Google Visualization API Essentials

Make sense of your data: make it visual with the
Google Visualization API

Traci L. Ruthkoski

BIRMINGHAM - MUMBAI

Google Visualization API Essentials

First published: April 2013

Production Reference: 1080413

Published by Packt Publishing Ltd.
Livery Place
35 Livery Street
Birmingham B3 2PB, UK.

ISBN 978-1-84969-436-0

www.packtpub.com

Cover Image by Faiz Fattohi (faizfattohi@gmail.com)

About the Reviewers

Louis-Guillaume Carrier-Bédard has been working for the last 9 years with Oracle technologies. Developments in the private and public sectors have helped him to build a solid background and renown in the Oracle APEX community. Louis-Guillaume received an honorable mention from Google Security for reporting security vulnerabilities; he appears on Google's Hall of Fame.

Louis-Guillaume is Oracle APEX Development Director at SIE-Solutions and CTO of newMarket. He is an adventurer who seeks new challenges to quench his thirst for knowledge.

He has worked as Technical Reviewer of the book *Oracle Application Express Forms Converter* (http://www.packtpub.com/oracle-application-express-forms-converter/book).

> I would like to say thank you to Michelle, the woman with whom I share my life. Thank you Bruno-Pierre, Stéphane, and Éric for the fun we had working on many projects.

Christophe Van Gysel (http://chri.stophr.be) is a Computer Scientist active in the Drupal community where he maintains and contributes to several projects. Beyond Drupal, he is also experienced in Distributed Systems and Machine Learning. In his spare time, Christophe specializes in Web Security research. He has participated in various white hat hacker programs.

He is the author and maintainer of Visualization API (http://drupal.org/project/visualization), an actively used module for Drupal that provides a robust and easy accessible way to visualize data. It supports, but is not limited to, the Google Visualization API.

Thomas Schäfer, who is a Former German Air Force Captain (academic degree), lives in Erftstadt, small city near Cologne, Germany.

He is an IT Pro since 2003. As a developer at Questback GmbH (Enterprise Feedback Software Company), he has worked on PHP, Javascript, MySQL, jQuery, and MooTools. He is also proficient with other technologies such as VisualBasic, C#, JAVA, Ruby, Python, PostgresSQL, NoSQL, ExtJS, GoogleVis API, and NodeJS. He has also worked in CSS Responsive Design using Compass.

He is 46 years old, married, and has two children.

www.PacktPub.com

Support files, eBooks, discount offers and more

You might want to visit www.PacktPub.com for support files and downloads related to your book.

Did you know that Packt offers eBook versions of every book published, with PDF and ePub files available? You can upgrade to the eBook version at www.PacktPub.com and as a print book customer, you are entitled to a discount on the eBook copy. Get in touch with us at service@packtpub.com for more details.

At www.PacktPub.com, you can also read a collection of free technical articles, sign up for a range of free newsletters and receive exclusive discounts and offers on Packt books and eBooks.

http://PacktLib.PacktPub.com

Do you need instant solutions to your IT questions? PacktLib is Packt's online digital book library. Here, you can access, read and search across Packt's entire library of books.

Why Subscribe?

- Fully searchable across every book published by Packt
- Copy and paste, print and bookmark content
- On demand and accessible via web browser

Free Access for Packt account holders

If you have an account with Packt at www.PacktPub.com, you can use this to access PacktLib today and view nine entirely free books. Simply use your login credentials for immediate access.

This book is dedicated to my mentor, Daniel E. Atkins III, the father of cyberinfrastructure and a lover of all things Google.

Table of Contents

Preface   **1**

Chapter 1: Tools and Setup   **7**

Knowledge prerequisites   **7**

Skill summary   8

System requirements   8

Interacting with Google Visualization Tools   **8**

Charts for Google Spreadsheets   9

Getting started – creating a new spreadsheet   9

Fusion Tables   11

Getting started – creating a new Fusion Table   11

Scripting code   12

Code Playground   13

Debugging tools   15

Console   15

Gadget Editor   16

Summary   **18**

Chapter 2: Anatomy of a Visualization   **19**

Common structure   **19**

Apps Script   21

Forms   21

Framework   22

Fusion Tables   23

Scripting code   24

HTML Framework   25

Technique options   25

Categories of visualizations   **26**

Static   27

Interactive	27
Dashboards	27
Events	29
Time-based charts	31
Summary	**33**
Chapter 3: Spreadsheets, Charts, and Fusion Tables	**35**
Spreadsheets	**36**
Creating a chart	36
The Chart Editor	38
Chart types	39
Reopening the Chart Editor	40
Chart styles	40
Using Apps Script	41
Framework	41
Scripting console	42
Fusion Tables	**46**
Importing or creating data	46
Data management	48
Editing rows	48
Modifying columns	49
Adding a formula	50
Views	50
New look in Fusion Tables	51
Merging tables	52
Creating a visualization	52
Non-map visualizations	53
A simple line graph	53
Experimental charts	54
Mapping features	55
Geocoding	55
Cell formatting	60
Summary	**64**
Chapter 4: Basic Charts	**65**
Programming concepts	**66**
Variables	66
Number	67
Boolean	67
String	67
Array	68
Equation	69
Functions	70
Classes (and objects)	71
Libraries	71
Commenting	72
Spacing/format	73

Visualization API common Framework	**73**
Load API modules	73
Apps Script Wrapper	80
A basic visualization	**82**
Code Playground	83
Apps Script	86
Summary	**88**
Chapter 5: Formatting Charts	**89**
Static	**90**
Spreadsheets	90
Fusion Tables	90
Chart Editor	92
Filters	92
API	93
Colors and fonts: Inline	93
Colors and fonts: Cascading Style Sheets	95
Views	96
DataTable formatters	99
Dynamic or interactive	**106**
Animated transitions	106
Dashboards and controls	107
Chart Editor for users	107
Summary	**107**
Chapter 6: Data Manipulation and Sources	**109**
Preparing data	**110**
Google Refine – importing data	110
Google Refine – Facets	111
Google Refine – clean and supplement	112
Google Refine – export options	114
Architecture and data modification	**115**
Protocol	115
Visualization API data capabilities	117
Group and join	118
Spreadsheets	124
Forms	124
API	125
Fusion Tables – API	126
Data sources for Charts	**126**
Spreadsheets	126
Preparation	126
Query	129

Fusion Tables	132
Preparation	132
Query	133
Chart Tools Query Language	138
Build your own data source	139
Summary	**140**
Chapter 7: Dashboards, Controls, and Events	**141**
Architecture	**142**
HTML framework	142
API framework	143
ControlWrapper	144
ChartWrapper	144
Dashboards	**149**
Controls	150
StringFilter	150
NumberRangeFilter	156
CategoryFilter	158
ChartRangeFilter	160
Controls with dependencies	161
Programmatic control	163
Global variables	165
Transition animation	**170**
Programmatic switch	173
User interface toggle	173
Create button	174
Button behavior	174
Chart editor for users	**176**
Summary	**179**
Chapter 8: Advanced Charts	**181**
Time-based charts	**181**
Motion chart	182
Spreadsheets	186
Code	188
Annotated timeline	190
Spreadsheets	191
Code	192
Maps	**195**
geochart versus geomap	195
The region option	196
The marker option	196
geochart	197
The ISO 3166 standard	197
Spreadsheets	198
Code	199

geomap   201
  Code   202
Map API   203
Your own visualization   **203**
Summary   **205**
Chapter 9: Publishing Options   **207**
  Sharing   **207**
  Private sharing   208
  Public sharing   211
  Publishing   **211**
  Spreadsheets   212
  Fusion Tables   214
  Apps Script   215
    Publishing basics   215
    Embedded in a Spreadsheet   217
  App Engine   217
    App Engine Launcher and SDK   217
    Eclipse plugin   218
    Integrated Development Environments in the Cloud (IDEs)   220
    More APIs   222
  A word on security   **223**
  Summary   **224**
Index   **225**

Preface

Visualization is a key component of analytics in both public and private organizations. The ability to view and even manipulate data visually is quickly becoming commonplace. Chart Tools, also known as the Visualization API, are powerful tools with low barriers to entry and are capable of impressive results with very little development time. Learning the Google Visualization API is also a helpful introduction to the larger collection of Google APIs.

What this book covers

Chapter 1, Tools and Setup, shows an overview of the various tools that can be used to create visualizations, from beginner to advanced levels. The purpose here is to explain the multiple approaches of using the API through different tools.

Chapter 2, Anatomy of a Visualization, describes the common high-level architecture that covers all methods of working with the Visualization API. This chapter also discusses the integrated nature of using the Visualization, Maps, and Fusion Tools APIs.

Chapter 3, Spreadsheet Charts and Fusion Tables, discusses becoming familiar with Fusion Tables and Google Spreadsheets user interfaces for chart creation and offers an easy to understand foundation from which advanced examples can be built.

Chapter 4, Basic Charts, dives deeper into the coding methods for the Visualization API. The examples are illustrated from beginner to advanced levels through examining each in Spreadsheets, Fusion Tables, and finally the code.

Chapter 5, Formatting Charts, shows formatting and style options for both tables and charts.

Chapter 6, Data Manipulation and Sources, describes methods of data sourcing for all visualization approaches. Techniques for querying and displaying data are also discussed.

Chapter 7, Dashboards, Controls, and Events, discusses user dashboards and controls. Dashboards and controls allow for user interactivity with the visualization.

Chapter 8, Advanced Charts, covers advanced topics in visualization with Google tools. Also included is further instruction on the use of Fusion Tables specifically for map data generation. The last section of the chapter will give a brief overview on how to build a fully custom virtualization.

Chapter 9, Publishing Options, discusses how, similar to multiple development options for Google Visualization, there are also multiple ways to share charts with others. This chapter presents common methods for publishing and sharing visualizations.

What you need for this book

Very little is required to get started. At the bare minimum, a Google account (free) and some experience working with HTML is expected. For advanced topics, knowledge of the basic programming concepts as well as some JavaScript experience is ideal.

The Google Visualization API does not require software to be installed on your computer. It is possible to perform all the development through an HTML5/SVG-capable web browser. However, for developers already familiar with common development environments such as Eclipse, it is also possible to develop for the Visualization API from these applications.

Who this book is for

This book will show you how to create web-ready data visualizations using Google's infrastructure. From casual Spreadsheets users to web developers, this book provides readers with both novice and advanced examples. Anyone with a need to dynamically visualize data on a website will benefit from reading this book.

Conventions

In this book, you will find a number of styles of text that distinguish between different kinds of information. Here are some examples of these styles, and an explanation of their meaning.

Code words in text, database table names, folder names, filenames, file extensions, pathnames, dummy URLs, user input, and Twitter handles are shown as follows: "Fusion Tables allows uploading of spreadsheets, delimited text files (.csv, .tsv, or .txt), and Keyhole Markup Language files (.kml) as table sources."

A block of code is set as follows:

```
function drawVisualization() {
  // Create and populate the data table.
  var data = google.visualization.arrayToDataTable([
    ['Age', 'Male', 'Female', 'Both Sexes'],
    ['Under 5 years',    94100,        91787,        185887],
    ['5 to 9 years',     84122,        81955,        166077],
```

When we wish to draw your attention to a particular part of a code block, the relevant lines or items are set in bold:

```
function drawVisualization() {
  // Create and populate the data table.
  var data = google.visualization.arrayToDataTable([
    ['Age', 'Male', 'Female', 'Both Sexes'],
    ['Under 5 years',    94100,        91787,        185887],
    ['5 to 9 years',     84122,        81955,        166077],
```

New terms and **important words** are shown in bold. Words that you see on the screen, in menus or dialog boxes for example, appear in the text like this: "Create the spreadsheet in Google Drive by selecting **Create | Spreadsheet**."

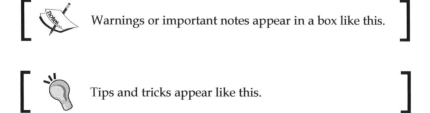

Warnings or important notes appear in a box like this.

Tips and tricks appear like this.

Reader feedback

Feedback from our readers is always welcome. Let us know what you think about this book—what you liked or may have disliked. Reader feedback is important for us to develop titles that you really get the most out of.

To send us general feedback, simply send an e-mail to feedback@packtpub.com, and mention the book title via the subject of your message.

If there is a topic that you have expertise in and you are interested in either writing or contributing to a book, see our author guide on www.packtpub.com/authors.

Customer support

Now that you are the proud owner of a Packt book, we have a number of things to help you to get the most from your purchase.

Downloading the example code

You can download the example code files for all Packt books you have purchased from your account at http://www.packtpub.com. If you purchased this book elsewhere, you can visit http://www.packtpub.com/support and register to have the files e-mailed directly to you.

Errata

Although we have taken every care to ensure the accuracy of our content, mistakes do happen. If you find a mistake in one of our books—maybe a mistake in the text or the code—we would be grateful if you would report this to us. By doing so, you can save other readers from frustration and help us improve subsequent versions of this book. If you find any errata, please report them by visiting http://www.packtpub.com/submit-errata, selecting your book, clicking on the **errata submission form** link, and entering the details of your errata. Once your errata are verified, your submission will be accepted and the errata will be uploaded on our website, or added to any list of existing errata, under the Errata section of that title. Any existing errata can be viewed by selecting your title from http://www.packtpub.com/support.

Piracy

Piracy of copyright material on the Internet is an ongoing problem across all media. At Packt, we take the protection of our copyright and licenses very seriously. If you come across any illegal copies of our works, in any form, on the Internet, please provide us with the location address or website name immediately so that we can pursue a remedy.

Please contact us at copyright@packtpub.com with a link to the suspected pirated material.

We appreciate your help in protecting our authors, and our ability to bring you valuable content.

Questions

You can contact us at questions@packtpub.com if you are having a problem with any aspect of the book, and we will do our best to address it.

1
Tools and Setup

It may come as a surprise to learn that using Google Visualization (Chart) Tools requires very little prior knowledge. One of the most satisfying aspects of working with this set of tools is the ease of leveraging a cloud platform. In other words, there is no requirement for high performance personal hardware and software setup that requires constant care and feeding on a laptop or desktop. While not ideal, it is even possible to develop projects from a tablet interface. In addition, with the interactive nature of the environment, real-time programming capability is a big plus during development.

In this chapter, the following topics are covered:

- Knowledge prerequisites
- Interacting with Google Visualization Tools

Knowledge prerequisites

With Google Visualization Tools, a developer with knowledge of HTML5 and some JavaScript can utilize approximately 90 percent of the functionality of the **Application Programming Interface (API)**. Some methods of creating visualizations do not even require writing code at all, but instead rely on the **Graphic User Interface (GUI)** of common Google Drive (previously known as Google Docs) tools. The remaining 10 percent of the functionality comes from the ability to interface with custom data sources. Google often makes its Java Libraries, in this case the Data Source Libraries, available for developers to use. A developer requiring such a capability can build custom data source connectors to a database on a web server. However, data connectors provided in the Visualization API, including communications through a SQL-like query language and jQuery, are generally adequate for most visualization projects.

Skill summary

To work in depth with the Visualization APIs, the following programming skills are highly recommended:

- HTML5
- JavaScript
- Java (specific uses only)

System requirements

In short, the Visualization API requires very little beyond a text editor and Internet access to create visualizations. However, additional tools make development much easier. Suggested tools or services when working with the Visualization API are as follows:

- A service or web server to host HTML pages
- A Google account with Google Drive activated (`https://drive.google.com/start`)

A Google account is required for the purposes of this book. Without a Google account, many of the tutorials and examples will not work properly.

Interacting with Google Visualization Tools

The key to understanding and then navigating the Google tool options is to first understand that everything is designed with integration in mind. In fact, much of Google's environment is already integrated to some degree. In this respect, the Google environment is truly an ecosystem of tools and capabilities. Some tools are focused on users that do not want to write code to create visualizations, while other tools allow a seasoned programmer to manipulate data with the API in very creative ways. The rest of this chapter is dedicated to an overview of the tools that are most commonly used as entry points for creating Google visualizations.

Charts for Google Spreadsheets

For anyone new to creating data visualizations with Google tools or those who are lacking in programming abilities, Google Spreadsheets is the ideal starting point. Spreadsheets allow developers at any experience level to easily create a wide variety of visualizations from Google's Spreadsheet platform through a point-and-click user interface. The primary limitation to this method is the lack of style and data formatting flexibility.

Fast facts: Google Spreadsheets Charts

- **Experience level**: Beginner to intermediate
- **Programming languages**: Google CodeScript (not required)
- **Advantages**: Easy to use, fast deployment, and code not required
- **Limitations**: Style options, data format flexibility, and scaling limits
- **Documentation**: http://www.google.com/google-d-s/spreadsheets/

Getting started – creating a new spreadsheet

Once logged in to Google Drive, create a chart using Google Spreadsheets. Create the spreadsheet in Google Drive by selecting **Create | Spreadsheet**.

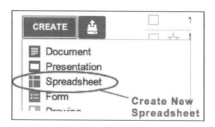

In the newly created spreadsheet, copy and paste, or otherwise enter the data to be visualized. Advanced methods of data import and manipulation can also be accomplished using the built-in scripting capabilities of Google Docs or through the Spreadsheets API. It is important to note that when using Spreadsheets to create charts, data must be arranged according to the requirement of the chart. To select a chart and in turn learn about its data formatting requirements, first insert the chart into the spreadsheet by selecting **Insert | Chart...** from the menu tab options.

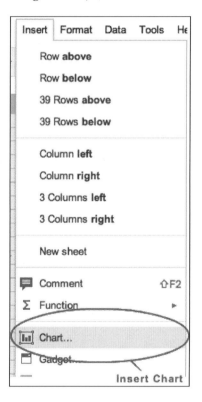

To select the appropriate chart for your data, the Spreadsheet Chart Editor detects the current data layout and then attempts to determine the correct chart selection. Further selection and customization techniques for charts in Google Spreadsheets are covered in *Chapter 3, Spreadsheets, Charts, and Fusion Tables*.

Fusion Tables

Google Fusion Tables is a tool primarily focused on geospatial visualization, and is available through logging in to Google Drive. If map visualization is desired, Fusion Tables is an ideal tool due to its built-in geocoding capabilities, recognition of standard marker names, and HTML-ready information windows. Fusion Tables is also capable of producing other charts such as line, bar, pie, scatter, and timelines. As a rapidly evolving application, Fusion Tables also presents a variety of experimental features still in testing. Opportunities to experiment with the latest features can be found by selecting the link, **View in Experimental**, at the top of the browser window, as shown in the following screenshot. Fusion Tables accepts a variety of import formats, including CSV, KML, ODS, XLS, and Google Spreadsheets.

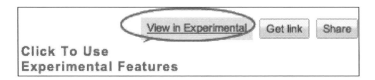

Fast facts: Google Fusion Tables

- Experience level: Beginner to intermediate
- Programming languages: Some HTML
- Advantages: Maps applications, scaling capacity, bulk data handling
- Limitations: Chart selection, style customization
- Documentation: http://www.google.com/ fusiontables/

Getting started – creating a new Fusion Table

To build a Fusion Tables visualization, create a new Table from the **Google Drive Create** tab. An alternative method to open the Fusion Table application is to visit http://www.google.com/fusiontables/ and click on the button.

In addition to manual entry, Fusion Tables allows Google Spreadsheets or a local file to be imported as data. Fusion Tables allows uploading of spreadsheets, delimited text files (`.csv`, `.tsv`, or `.txt`), and Keyhole Markup Language files (`.kml`) as table sources.

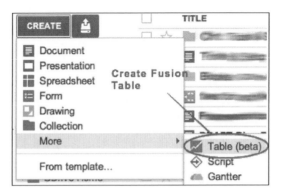

For users with enterprise class map visualization needs, Google offers a for-fee service, Google Map Engine. Map Engine runs with the same services that support regular maps and earth, but are backed by Google's compute cloud for high performance mapping capabilities. Unlike Fusion Tables, Map Engine does not include visualization methods other than map-based options.

You can find more information on Google Map Engine at `http://www.google.com/enterprise/mapsearth/products/mapsengine.html`.

Scripting code

HTML code that contains references to the Visualization API (or any Google API for that matter) can be run locally, or hosted by any web hosting service. However, one of the easiest methods is to simply use Google's own App Engine to host visualizations. App Engine is a scalable web hosting environment that can be linked to development platforms, such as Eclipse, which offers a seamless web development workflow when using the Google Web Tools plugin for Eclipse.

Google App Engine currently offers developers 10 free, hosted applications, with additional capacity available through pay-as-you-go fees. For developers looking to experiment with Google APIs, including the Visualization API, App Engine paired with Eclipse is a capable yet affordable platform. However, for developers not quite ready to build complex applications, Google maintains a free, real-time API sandbox for development use. Additionally, for developers who are not quite so advanced at this time, online IDE environments are easy and affordable for code development. They also generally offer an automated connection to cloud hosting services, such as Google App Engine.

Fast facts: Scripting code using the Visualization API

- **Experience level**: Intermediate to advanced
- **Advantages**: Full customization and scalability
- **Limitations**: Developer experience
- **Web hosting**: Optional but Recommended
- **Documentation**: `https://developers.google.com/chart/`

You can find more information at the following links:

- **Google App Engine**: `https://developers.google.com/appengine/`
- **Eclipse**: `http://www.eclipse.org/`
- **Google Web Tools plugin for Eclipse**: `https://developers.google.com/web-toolkit/`

Code Playground

Code Playground is Google's real-time AJAX code development sandbox for discovering, learning, and testing Google API code. The Playground is updated regularly, with feature updates as well as new API examples. It's worth the effort to check this space regularly to see if something new has been released. The Visualization API release notes are also a very helpful resource for this task.

The sandbox has a tree-structured **Navigation** window in the upper-left corner of the page. Depending on which API example is highlighted, sample code and corresponding live output are displayed in the **Edit Code** and **Output** windows respectively. Code in the **Edit Code** window can be edited in real time, with changes appearing in the **Output** window after the ▶ Run Code button is clicked.

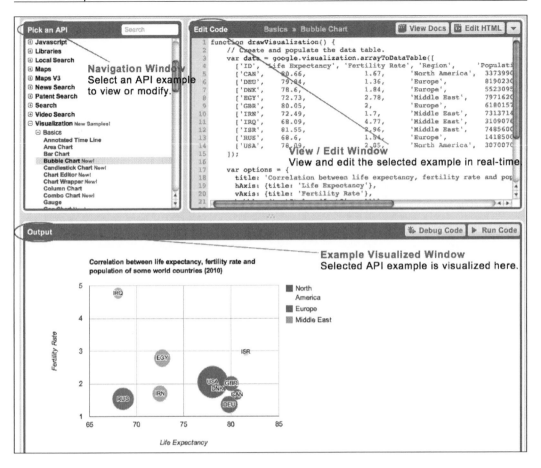

Code Playground also allows developers to save modifications to existing API examples within the environment. If a developer wants to save the state of HTML displayed in the **Edit Code** window, there are options to **Save** as well as **Export** to view a live version. When logged in with a Google account, the **Save** option saves the current code state to the Code Playground itself. **Export** saves the current state to a Google App Engine instance that can be referenced by the ID contained in the URL.

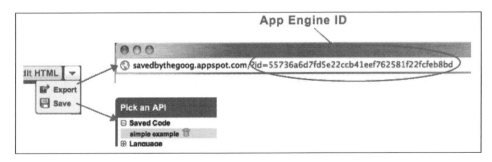

Finally, to view Google's documentation and other resources for the currently highlighted API, select the  View Docs button. To edit all HTML encapsulating the API calls, click on the Edit HTML button.

You can find more information at the following links:

- **Google Code Playground**: `http://code.google.com/apis/ajax/playground/`

- **Visualization API Release Notes**: `https://developers.google.com/chart/interactive/docs/release_notes`

Debugging tools

A clear advantage to developing Google APIs in the Code Playground environment is the integrated debugging mode. Code Playground makes use of the Firebug Lite web development tool. To activate debug mode, click on the Debug Code button. (Note that Chrome users can also use Chrome's built-in JavaScript console.)

> Firebug Lite
> `http://getfirebug.com/firebuglite`

Console

Debug mode offers several methods of testing and debugging code. To toggle between the **DOM** and **Console** views, select the appropriate tab. To clear the console, select **Clear**. To get more information on Firebug and Firebug Lite, click on the bug icon.

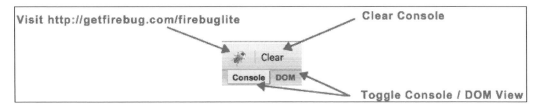

A feature of Firebug Lite that can be easily missed is the **Firebug Lite Settings** window. To view **Firebug Lite Settings**, select **Options** in the bottom-right corner of the Playground interface. To configure the debugging environment as desired, check or uncheck the options in the list.

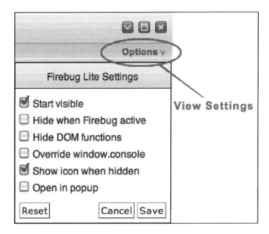

Additionally, the command line offers yet another method of testing and debugging the code in the Code Playground environment. Developers can set variables, test scenarios, and otherwise debug code through a command line real-time input. The resulting output, depending on the entries to the command line, is viewed in the debug **Console** window.

> >>> Type in additional Javascript to debug your application, or a variable's name to print out its value.

Gadget Editor

If the end purpose of the visualization is to be embedded in a Google Calendar, Gmail, Sites, or other application, encapsulating the visualization within a Google Gadget wrapper can be helpful. A simple method of creating a visualization intended for a Gadget is to first edit the API code, with HTML included, in the Code Playground, and then cut and paste in between the appropriate tags in the Google Gadget Editor.

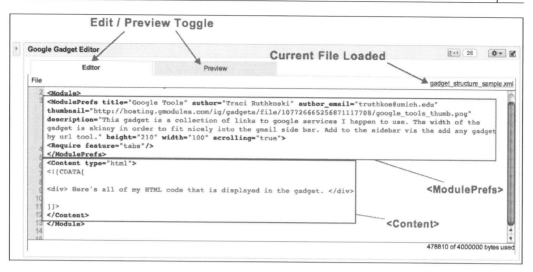

The Gadget Editor itself is a simple HTML editing interface with a preview mode included. A Google Gadget is comprised of two major sections within a set of `<Module>` tags. The `<ModulePrefs>` tag contains information about the gadget, including the title, author name, thumbnail location (in the Gadget Gallery at `http://www.google.com/ig/directory`), and description. To publicly publish a gadget in the Gadget Gallery, the `ModulePrefs` section must be laid out according to Google's standards (`http://www.google.com/ig/submit`), as well as follow Google's terms of service (`https://developers.google.com/gadgets/terms-nc`).

To insert content, place the desired gadget's content to be displayed between the `<Content>` tags. The general format for content is HTML, but JavaScript can also be used. To save a Gadget, select **File | Save**. The gadget is now stored on Google servers, but is only available to those with the link and not available publicly. To publish a gadget to the public Gadget Gallery, select **File | Publish** from the menu options.

Just as the newly created gadget is stored on Google infrastructure when using Gadget Editor, images and other content can also be stored in the same location for the gadget's use. Select **File | Upload** to upload images for the gadget's use. The image URL resulting from the upload, usually of the form `http://hosting.gmodules.com/ig/gadgets/file/12345.../filename.png`, can then be used to reference the image in the gadget HTML.

Fast facts: Gadget Editor

- **Experience level**: Intermediate to advanced
- **Advantages**: Free Google hosting available and embedding in web pages and apps
- **Limitations**: Developer experience
- **Documentation**: `https://developers.google.com/gadgets/`

WARNING

The future of Google Gadgets is unclear at the time of publishing. Many features of Gadgets are being absorbed by other Google services. However, they are still available as a platform for development.

You can find more information on Google Gadget Editor at `https://developers.google.com/gadgets/docs/tools#GGE`.

Summary

It is important to remember that there are multiple methods of creating visualizations when working with Google tools. A developer may choose to select one method over another, depending on the complexity and features required by the visualization. It is also important to observe that Google is actively adding functionality to the API collections as well as the user interface applications. Regular visits to the API documentation and Code Playground will generally yield new methods of visualization creation. In summary, at the time of this publication, visualizations using Google tools can be created with:

- Google Spreadsheets
- Google Fusion Tables
- Custom applications that reference the Google Visualization API, created in Code Playground or a third-party platform (for example, Eclipse)

Architecture and types of visualization options is the topic of the next chapter.

2
Anatomy of a Visualization

There are multiple approaches with which a developer can work with the Visualization API, so it is helpful to give an architectural overview of various workflows. This chapter describes the common high-level architecture that underlies the most common methods of working with the Visualization API. In this chapter, we will also discuss the integration of various aspects of Visualization (Chart), Maps, and Fusion Tables. These three APIs often work together to allow developers varying in expertise to build complex, dynamic visualizations with relatively little effort. The final section of this chapter is dedicated to outlining the types of visualizations.

In this chapter we will cover the following:

- API architecture overview
- Interaction with other APIs
- Visualization types

Common structure

At its core, the Visualization API acts as a bridge between a data source that contains data and an HTML page displaying the data. Regardless of platform, the Visualization API follows the same architecture as other Google API products. Methods to use for Google APIs consequently also follow the same general structure as APIs from other application providers such as Flickr or Facebook. For most APIs, including the Google APIs, the JavaScript namespace structure is as follows:

```
application.category.function(variables)
```

For example, to create a new pie chart with the Google Visualization API, the corresponding code would be as follows:

```
new google.visualization.PieChart(document.getElementById('visualizat
ion'));
```

For non-code based platforms, such as Spreadsheets and Fusion Tables, the user interface that encapsulates the Visualization API is designed to enhance the strengths of a particular tool set for a wide spectrum of users. For example, Fusion Tables is primarily focused on map visualization by inclusion of geocoding capabilities, as well as specific format standards to simplify map overlay deployment. Similarly, Spreadsheets primarily functions as a spreadsheet application, but is capable of some chart visualizations through an integrated graphic user interface. The integration of the Visualization API in these cases is primarily for the enhancement of the capabilities of the parent application. On the other hand, developing applications directly with the Visualization API affords the developer a higher level of freedom in design than either Spreadsheets or Fusion Tables.

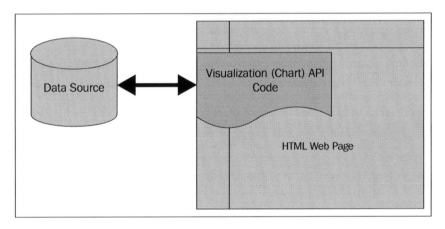

Spreadsheets integrates much of the Visualization API into an easy-to-use graphic user interface within the Spreadsheets application itself. Data manipulation and data input can be done programmatically through the Spreadsheets Forms feature, Apps Script, or even the Spreadsheet API. Each method is likely to affect chart renderings, as they offer opportunities to collect, move, format, and delete data in methodical, repeatable ways.

 You can find more information about Google Spreadsheets Documentation at http://www.google.com/google-d-s/spreadsheets/.

Apps Script

Chart rendering is one of the many uses of Google's scripting platform, Apps Script. Initially it was included only within Google Spreadsheets and Documents. Apps Script has since been elevated to a standalone filetype in Google Drive. The purpose of Apps Script is to allow a user to programmatically manipulate data, or even the Google document interface itself in Google Drive. Apps Script projects created in Google Drive documents can also be launched as applications through the Apps Script development platform. Introducing the creation of web forms, filter controls, and other web interfaces outside the Google Drive environment enhances the interactive, data-driven chart potential.

 You can find more information about Google Apps Script Documentation at `https://developers.google.com/apps-script/`.

Forms

Another method available to input data into Spreadsheets is through the Forms functionality. Launch the Forms configuration tool by selecting **Insert | Form** from the Spreadsheet menu tabs. The resulting survey-style form can then be embedded into a website iFrame, or can be a standalone web page hosted by Google. Forms are not intended to facilitate two-way interaction with data, but are only a method of inputting data into spreadsheets. Note that when a form is created to bring data into a spreadsheet, the format of the spreadsheet is automatically configured to collect the timestamp of each entry submission in the first column. Form question responses are collected in the order they are asked and stored in subsequent columns. When the form is deleted, the first column returns to its default state and the **Form** tab disappears.

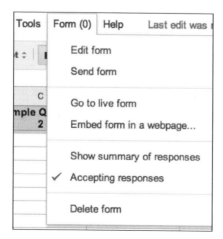

You can find more information about Google Forms Documentation at http://www.google.com/google-d-s/forms/.

Framework

The combined result of Spreadsheets and its compatible technologies is a simplified yet capable web platform. A developer may choose to interact with visualization tools through the Spreadsheets GUI, Apps Script, or JavaScript (most often inside the <script> tags). Multiple methods of data manipulation can also be programmatically invoked. These methods include using Forms, Apps Script, Visualization API, or the Spreadsheets API itself. The charts created in Spreadsheets can be displayed as embedded in an iFrame, standalone App Engine web application, or custom application.

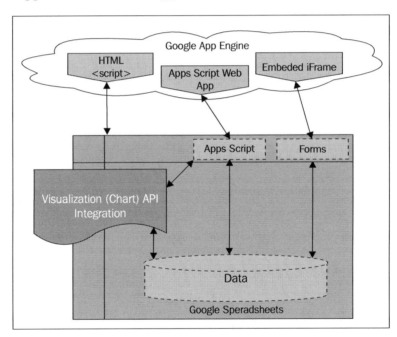

Fusion Tables

Similar to Spreadsheets, Fusion Tables creates an easy-to-use environment in which visualizations can be created without writing code. However, Fusion Tables is primarily focused on visualization of map data and integrates the map and chart API functionalities with a table optimized for map data. Maps rendered in Fusion Tables can be displayed in an embedded iFrame, standalone HTML link, or as part of a larger custom application.

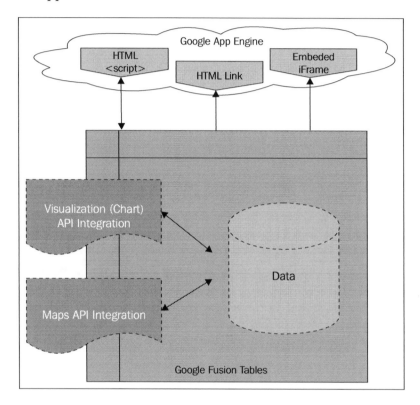

 You can find more information about Google Fusion Tables Documentation at http://www.google.com/fusiontables.

Scripting code

Writing applications wrapped in HTML and directly manipulating the Visualization API is the most versatile method of chart creation. Consequently, this method can often be the most labor intensive and will require some HTML and JavaScript programming experience. The following diagram depicts the HTML page residing in Google App Engine. While this is a possible hosting location, it is not a requirement to publish code that references the Google APIs in Google App Engine. A key difference between the Spreadsheets or Fusion Tables approach and scripting custom code is that the data resides outside of the development platform. Both Spreadsheets and Fusion Tables encapsulate their data within the development platform, where a custom application using the Visualization API must interact with the data through various API methods. The Visualization API itself contains a simple set of programmatic data manipulation and retrieval calls using `google.visualization.dataclass` of functions. Other APIs may also be leveraged to manage data if the hosting application also has an API. For example, Spreadsheets API or Fusion Tables API can be used along side the Visualization API in the same application. One method of using Spreadsheets and Fusion Tables data programmatically within the Visualization API framework is to use the SQL-like language provided in the Visualization API. This SQL-like language is named Query and functions from its class can be called by the method `google.visualization.query`.

 You can find more information about Google Chart Tools API Documentation at `https://developers.google.com/chart/`.

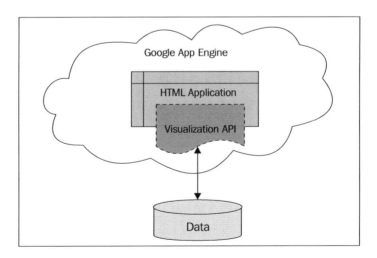

HTML Framework

The API use is not limited to just one section of the HTML document. For the purposes of the instructions in this book, Chart API visualizations will be included within the `<script>` tags of HTML code. As expected in HTML, the `<script>` tags are included inside the `<head>` tags. To place the code on an HTML page, a `<div>` tag names the ID in the `<body>` tag, which the visualization uses to create the chart on the page. General HTML styles for the browser window and visualization frame can be provided in the `<body>` tag definition by following normal HTML practices. The generalized structure of an application using the visualization API, including its HTML framework, is as follows:

```html
<html>
  <head>
    <script>
      API code goes here, including any libraries to be loaded.
    </script>
  </head>
  <body>
    <div id="chart_name_goes_here"</div>
  </body>
</html>
```

Downloading the example code

You can download the example code files for all Packt books you have purchased from your account at `http://www.packtpub.com`. If you purchased this book elsewhere, you can visit `http://www.packtpub.com/support` and register to have the files e-mailed directly to you.

Technique options

In the code inside the `<script>` tags, there are three primary methods in which the Visualization API can be invoked to draw charts. The most versatile of the three is `chart.draw()`. However, a drawback of using `chart.draw()` is that it requires explicit loading of the directories required for the particular visualization. Alternatively, `ChartWrapper` is an easier method to use, but trades ease of use for less flexibility when working with event handling. With almost the same functionality, `Draw.Chart()` is an even more compact version of `ChartWrapper`, and requires less code. However, `Draw.Chart()` further trades functionality for ease of use as `Draw.Chart()` is not capable of handling events.

Drawing techniques: chart.draw() versus ChartWrapper versus Draw.Chart()

You can find information about this at `https://developers.google.com/chart/interactive/docs/drawing_charts`.

Comparison: chart.draw() versus ChartWrapper versus Draw.Chart()

The following table compares the three drawing techniques:

Feature	chart.draw()	ChartWrapper	Draw.Chart()
Explicit control: Loading visualization libraries required	✓	✗	✗
Explicit control: Callback function needed for event handling and queries	✓	✗	✗
Functionality: Handles events	✓	✓	✗
Automated: Load visualization libraries	✗	✓	✓
Automated: Event handling and queries	✗	✓	✗

In general, the ChartWrapper method will suffice for most projects. Draw.Chart() can be used on projects that do not require event handling. A developer may choose to use the chart.draw() method, and will generally tend to do so if verbose event handling is required.

Categories of visualizations

Visualizations fall into two categories, static and interactive. Static visualizations are simply pictures that do not include controls or manipulation capabilities for the viewer. Conversely, an interactive visualization allows the viewer to manipulate data views, cause events, and otherwise have a dynamic interaction with the visualization.

Static

A static chart is a snapshot view of data. The viewer cannot manipulate the chart, other than viewing details through simple mouse-over windows. Chart types that generally fall into the Static category are as follows:

- Line charts
- Pie charts
- Bar graphs
- Candlestick charts
- Geography maps and charts
- Scatter plots
- Basic tables
- Tree maps
- Organizational charts

However, note that Static charts may be transformed into Interactive charts by adding dashboard controls, which is a topic covered in detail in *Chapter 7, Dashboards, Controls, and Events*.

Interactive

Interactive charts allow the viewer to manipulate the display properties of the chart's data. Often these visualizations are built from simpler static charts, with controls added to allow the viewer interaction. However, there are also charts that are capable of referencing a timeline to provide data representation over a given period of time. Interactive data observation over time can be accomplished by using either the motion chart or timeline chart. Also, advanced interactive map charts that are timeline driven can be rendered using the Maps API.

Dashboards

A dashboard is the inclusive name given to a set of controls presented to the viewer with which the viewer is able to manipulate the visualization in order to get his/her own desired views of the data. Dashboards usually include one or more filters to allow for end user data viewing control.

Filter by string

The string filtering option is equivalent to providing a contained search option to the chart's end user. Data displayed, in whatever chart format, will be restricted based on the string entered in the field. Results filtered by the string are real time.

Filter by number range

The number range slider allows the viewer to select a range of values from the dataset to display. The chart view will reflect the restriction of values set by the slider. Parameters set by the slider are real time.

Filter by chart range

The chart range slider allows users to select a smaller section of a larger chart in order to gain a more detailed view. The slider parameters are drag-and-drop on either side of the selected area. Rendering for the selected chart area is real time.

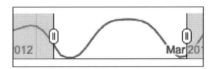

Programmatic filtering

The number range slider, combined with one or more preset button selections allows programmatic filtering of data into methods. The range of the slider itself is determined by the maximum and minimum values of the associated dataset. The text on the button is defined using HTML definitions within the `<body>` tag. The range of data viewed can be set by dragging the number range handles to the desired range, in the same way as manipulating a standard number range bar. The number range can also be configured by clicking on the preset button (the **Select range [15, 27]** button in the following screenshot), to set pre-configured values. Buttons can also be used to set the visualization properties.

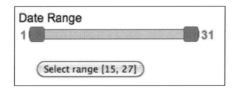

Filter by category

Category filters allow chart users to selectively view data based on categories presented in the drop-down menu. In the following example, books will only be viewed in the corresponding chart if they fall into the categories of **Non-Fiction** and **Biographies**. The categories presented for filtering are defined by specifying a column in the data table.

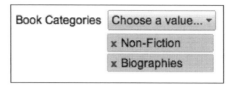

Filter by dependencies

The dependency filter allows data to be viewed in a drilldown method. Each subsequent set of options for selection is dependent on the previous drop-down selection. The data displayed on the visualization is pared down accordingly with each additional selection from the filter list. Similar to button definitions for programmatic filtering, the drop-down IDs for each filter are created inside the `<body>` tags and then referenced in the API script.

Events

In general application programming, event handling is a structured method of programmatically reacting to user interactions. Event handling is a key tool in the creation of interactive charts because it allows a variety of feedback opportunities to the user.

Selection and sort

It is possible to trigger events by making a selection on a table display. For example, selecting a row in a table can trigger a browser alert and message to the viewer of the chart. It is also possible to configure the title bar of a chart to sort data in a specified order. The corresponding chart visualization will display the data in the order that was sorted in the table. Similarly, a chart may be the source of a user click, with the corresponding table row being selected by the user's action.

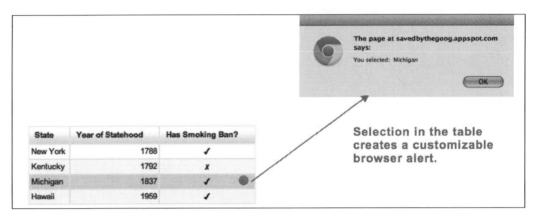

Ready for interaction

Visualizations can also be programmed to be rendered on the command of the viewer. For example, a button on an HTML page can be programmed to wait for a user click in order to initiate the rendering of a chart. The resulting actions after the button click may also set formatting parameters, initiate sending alert messages to the user, or even initiate additional events.

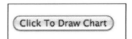

Error handling

Errors are a form of events, and all well-written applications should include some method of error handling. Google provides an error handling namespace included in the Visualization API. The `google.visualization.errors` namespace provides static functions that allow the developer to display error messages to the user, if necessary.

You can find Error Handling Documentation at https://developers.google.com/chart/interactive/docs/reference#errordisplay.

Time-based charts

There are two types of visualizations intended to display data that changes over a period of time. These charts are the annotated timeline chart and the motion chart.

Annotated timeline charts

The annotated timeline chart is as its name describes, and it displays annotations of specific points on a line chart over time. Each annotation can be documented with detailing text, which appears in the right-most column. Moving a set of sliders across the bottom range viewer can specify a magnified view of a point in time on the timeline.

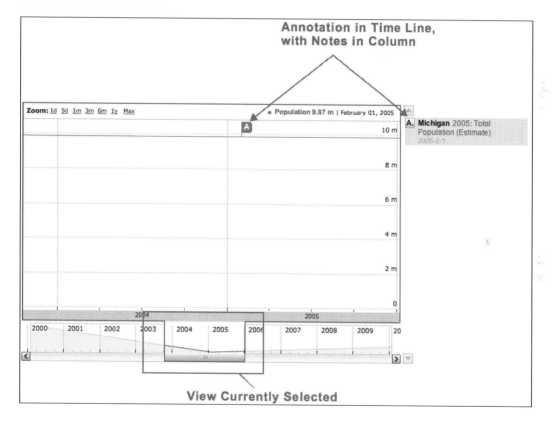

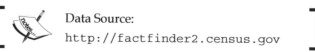

Data Source:
http://factfinder2.census.gov

Motion charts

The motion chart maps the changes of one or more variables over time on a defined axis. There are a number of user-defined controls available to manipulate the chart during viewing. The following example of a motion chart depicts the population of three U.S. states between the years 2000-2010. The segment of each state's population that is of age 18 and over is signified by the size of the motion trail. The bottom segment of each motion trail represents the population of each state under the age of 18. The upper portion of the motion trail signifies the total number of persons over the age of 18.

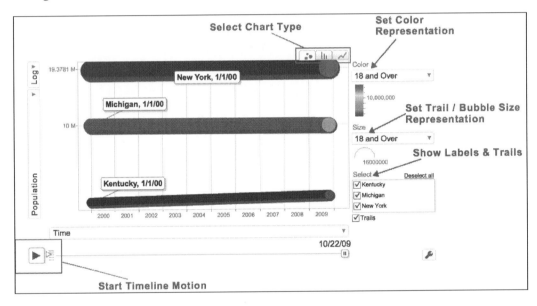

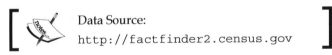

Data Source:
http://factfinder2.census.gov

Summary

The purpose of this chapter was to give an overview of several architectures available for creating chart visualizations. It must be understood that the architectures presented here are by no means exclusive to the options available to developers working within the Google API framework or even with the Visualization API. Rather it is more useful to view the preceding overview as of the most common architectures that can be used as a starting point for chart development. The integration capabilities are provided by Google enable creativity, but can also be limiting due to confusion of how and when to use combinations of methods. Missed opportunities to visualize data creatively can be common when there is a lack of understanding that two or more methods may need to be incorporated in order to provide the desired solution.

All visualizations, regardless of the tools used to create them, follow the same methodology. This methodology is inclusive of naming hierarchy as well as application structure. It is also the same or similar to other Google APIs and very often third-party API conventions. Basic understanding of recommended uses for the various capabilities of the Visualization API and partnering Google applications will help the developer make informed design decisions. Using the more familiar applications of Spreadsheets and Fusion Tables, and discussion on individual API charts are the topics of the next chapter.

3
Spreadsheets, Charts, and Fusion Tables

As a result of high demand for the Visualization API, Fusion Tables API, and Maps API functionalities, several applications have been developed by Google to provide a simple **graphic user interface (GUI)** on top of these common but fairly complex integrations. Fusion Tables and Google Spreadsheets provide application interfaces for chart creation, but ultimately rely on various underlying Google API infrastructure functionalities. Using the GUIs prior to direct API manipulation offers an easy-to-understand building block for learning the Visualization API.

In this chapter we will cover:

- Creating charts in Google Spreadsheets
- The Chart Editor
- Apps Script
- Creating charts in Google Fusion Tables
- Geocoding
- Markers, Lines, Areas, and Info Windows

Spreadsheets

For anyone who has used a generic spreadsheet application in the past, Google Spreadsheets becomes a natural starting point when learning about Google visualizations. Data entry, chart creation, and formula functionality in Google Spreadsheets is extremely similar to other generic spreadsheet applications. Yet, a significant difference between traditional spreadsheet charting applications and Google Spreadsheets is the ability to enhance capabilities by overlying Apps Scripts, and re-create and enhance the same chart with the Visualization API. Direct API access allows a developer to include advanced features such as style customization and dynamic manipulation of the data.

Spreadsheets are built from Google infrastructure, and thus inherit some dynamic capabilities from the Visualization API. These features are generally presented as static capabilities in Spreadsheets, and can only be modified if control has been offered through the GUI (for example, colors and fonts). Then, additional chart functionality can be implemented through the JavaScript language used to extend Google Apps, named Apps Script. It is also worth noting that the Spreadsheets application has its own API interface, which opens up entirely new opportunities to be used that are outside the scope of the Spreadsheets GUI application.

Creating a chart

To create a new spreadsheet, click on the **CREATE** button, or open an existing spreadsheet in Google Drive.

Enter data into the spreadsheet manually, or use the bulk import method. To import, select **File | Import...** from the Spreadsheets menu. The **Import file** dialogue will give a variety of import formatting options as well as data placement options within the existing or new spreadsheet.

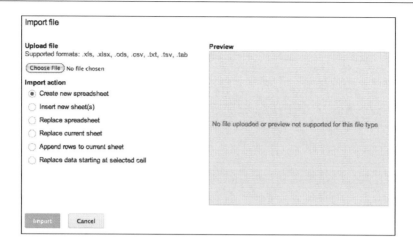

The data used in the following Spreadsheets example is the United States Census data, collected from the city of Chicago in 2010. The data lists the number of male and female individuals residing in the city of Chicago, divided by age group.

	A	B	C	D
1	Age	Male	Female	Both Sexes
2	Under 5 years	94100	91787	185887
3	5 to 9 years	84122	81955	166077
4	10 to 14 years	83274	81192	164466
5	15 to 19 years	91528	91405	182933
6	20 to 24 years	108407	114620	223027
7	25 to 29 years	134931	141208	276139
8	30 to 34 years	119828	119584	239412
9	35 to 39 years	100651	99857	200508
10	40 to 44 years	89957	87674	177631
11	45 to 49 years	85645	86217	171862
12	50 to 54 years	80838	86037	166875
13	55 to 59 years	68441	76170	144611
14	60 to 64 years	54592	63646	118238
15	65 to 69 years	37704	47366	85070
16	70 to 74 years	27787	38238	66025
17	75 to 79 years	20448	30252	50700
18	80 to 84 years	14637	24467	39104
19	85 to 89 years	7842	16548	24390
20	90 years and over	3340	9303	12643
21				

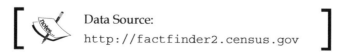

Data Source:
http://factfinder2.census.gov

With data populated in the spreadsheet, select **Insert | Chart...** from the menu options to create a visualization of the data.

The Chart Editor

In Google Spreadsheets, the Chart Editor appears when we open an existing chart to edit in the advanced mode. It is the interface for developing visualizations from within Google Spreadsheets.

Chart Editor offers three primary functions. These functions are as follows:

- **Configure data**: Sets which data from the table is actually used in the visualization
- **Chart type**: Line, bar, or pie
- **Style customization**: Colors, fonts, and titles

In the Chart Editor, the ability to define which data is used in the visualization is found under the **Start** tab, which also happens to be the default view when opening Chart Editor. In this tab, the spreadsheet cells to be included in the visualization are set in the **Data – Select ranges…** box. It is also possible to combine ranges, switch rows and columns, and set label/header information to be displayed in the visualization.

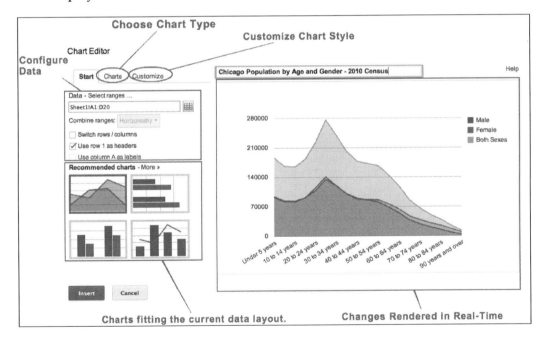

Chart types

Chart types are determined primarily in the **Charts** tab, but can also be set in the **Recommended charts** box in the **Start** tab. Depending on the configuration of the columns and rows in the spreadsheet, Spreadsheets will recommend the most suitable chart for the existing data's structure. If a desired type of chart does not correspond to the current data layout, it is necessary to learn about a chart's layout in order to configure the data appropriately. A chart that fits the current data configuration is represented by a colored thumbnail preview of itself. A chart that does not fit the current data layout will be represented as a grayed-out thumbnail preview of itself. Select the grayed-out thumbnail preview to view information on the required data layout for that particular visualization.

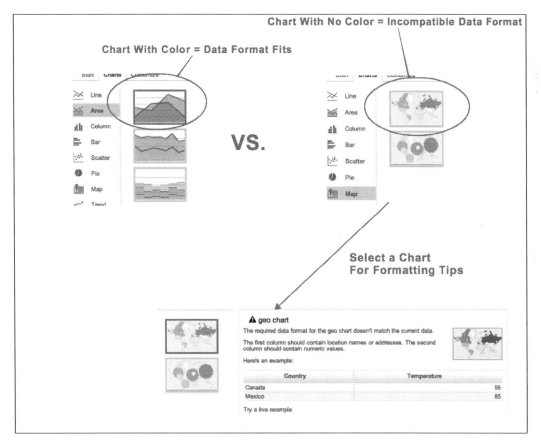

Reopening the Chart Editor

If additional detailed modifications to the chart are required beyond the quick edit funcionality, return to editing an existing visualization by selecting the **Advanced chart...** option in the drop-down menu on the chart itself.

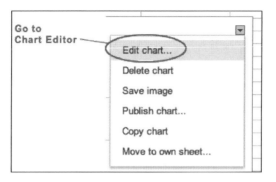

Chart styles

Basic formatting of a visualization can be accomplished in the **Customize** tab. The features available for customization are dependent on the type of chart, but generally always include abilities to create a title, placement, and font format for the chart's legend, and change the colors and fonts of various attributes.

The Visualization functionality from within Google Spreadsheets is fairly basic. However, additional capabilities can be implemented through the use of Google Apps Script.

Using Apps Script

Apps Script is a JavaScript-based platform for scripting customized features into a variety of Google applications. Apps Scripts are allowed to call Google APIs and thus can be used to manipulate various aspects of a handful of Google applications. Apps Script is also as much a script management platform as it is a script executable platform. Scripts can be embedded in the respective Google application or can be standalone files in Google Drive. Additionally, Apps Script is capable of launching the scripts as a standalone web application.

 You can find more information about Apps Script Documentation at `https://developers.google.com/apps-script/`.

Framework

The following is a list of the Apps Script compatible Google products. Apps Script can be used in:

- Spreadsheets
- Documents
- Google Drive
- Sites
- Google-Hosted Web Application
- Gmail
- Calendar

The advantage of using Apps Script is that it provides a single platform on which to mix Google application functionality. With this capability, it is possible to create a single, feature-rich application from many Google applications and services. For example, the 2010 Chicago Census chart could benefit from dynamic user-controlled filters on the **Male** or **Female** columns or the **Age** column. Apps Script can facilitate data retrieval from the Spreadsheet and a development platform from which user-defined filtering web applications can be launched. Apps Script web applications are stripped-down versions of Google App Engine applications, but they run on the App Engine infrastructure. The Apps Script framework is designed so that scripts can be easily deployed as web applications.

Scripting console

In Fusion Tables, creating new scripts and customizing scripts is done in the manager and editor options. Navigating to **Insert Tab | Script...** allows insertion of existing third-party scripts from the user community gallery. Gallery scripts can then be modified once they are placed in a new, Apps Script supportive Google file. Navigating through the **Tools Tab** options, **Tools | Script editor...** and **Tools | Script manager...** allows access to the script editing console and a management function for spreadsheets embedded in the Spreadsheets file respectively. The Apps Script development platform also opens as a separate tab in the browser window, in this case, separate from the **Spreadsheets** tab.

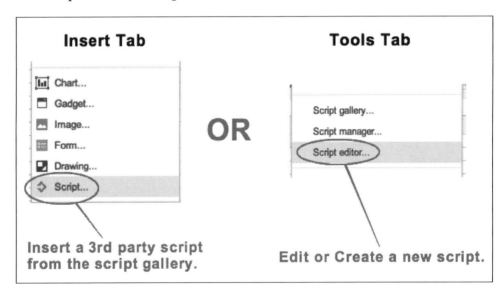

The Apps Script editor console is arranged in a project style, which also includes basic debugging and web app publishing capabilities. Code is entered in the code view or edit window for which a file of type Google Script (gs) is created. Scripts contained in the project are organized in the side column. The menu tab and console controls contain several of the same functions, allowing various workflow preferences while developing.

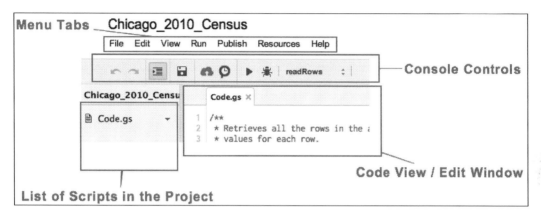

Testing functions

To test a function in your project, select the name of the function from the drop-down menu and then click on the arrow or run button. This capability is nice to have when it's difficult to determine a script error. Running each function separately is a good way to test if each one is working on its own. To select a function to test apart from other functions in a script, use the drop-down list in the console controls bar.

Clicking on the drop-down list will display functions in the script that can be run. Select a function in the list to test its functionality.

Debugging scripts

The console control button with a bug icon will put the console in debug mode when clicked.

Apps Script is also a development environment for Google web apps that make use of various Google APIs. The debug mode, in addition to inline syntax and function help, makes Apps Script a decent development platform for Google API based apps.

Event triggers

The purpose of triggers is to initiate an event, such as sending notifications via e-mail at a scheduled time, if a particular action on or about the spreadsheet has occurred. The clock icon in the controls console bar will initiate a dialog with the developer to add, modify, or remove event triggers from the script.

Types of events that can trigger script execution are as follows:

- Opening the spreadsheet itself
- When a script function has been run
- Time-driven events

Publishing as an App

The cloud button is used to publish an Apps Script to Google App Engine.

To publish, Apps Script requires saving and managing versions by navigating to **File | Manage Versions…**. After a version is saved, navigating to **Publish | Deploy as web app…** or clicking on the cloud button will initiate the web deployment dialog.

The versioning control and the user interface creation options are currently in the experimental phase and are both currently under the **File** tab. Google updates its services and applications regularly, so whenever an experimental feature is added, it will be marked as **EXPERIMENTAL!** within the application itself.

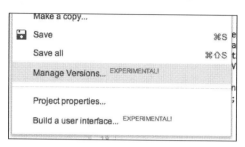

Apps Script is versatile in its abilities beyond scripting web apps using the APIs. It is also capable of acting as a medium for using the APIs to create customizations in Google applications themselves. The following is a short example of how Apps Script can be used for creating a custom spreadsheet menu item. The menu item created in this example is named `Launch App`. `Launch App` contains a drop-down list for a script function called `doGet`. To continually illustrate the usefulness of Apps Script when combined with the Google APIs, Apps Script compatible code will be provided throughout the remainder of this book for each topic.

```
functiononOpen() {
  /* Retrieves the active spreadsheet as a source */
  var sheet = SpreadsheetApp.getActiveSpreadsheet();

  /* Create the menu entry for a function */
  var entries = [{
    name : "Launch App",
    functionName : "doGet"
  }];
  /* Create the Spreadsheet Menu tab. */
  sheet.addMenu("Script Menu", entries);
};
```

Fusion Tables

Google Fusion Tables is a GUI application targeted towards providing a simple data source in combination with a host of standard visualization options. The biggest difference between Fusion Tables and Spreadsheets is that Fusion Tables is a visualization tool first, then a data source, and does not include much calculation functionality. Like Google Spreadsheets, Fusion Tables has its own accompanying API. The API is primarily focused on SQL-like capabilities and usage of Fusion Tables as a data source.

Importing or creating data

To create an empty table or import data into a table, use the method outlined in *Chapter 1, Tools and Setup*. Select **Create | Table** in Google Drive. The **Import new table** wizard will automatically open. Select the type of import or create an empty table. Alternatively, Fusion Tables offers a collection of public data tables that can also be imported. Data is also available in the form of existing user Fusion Tables that have been made available by the user community.

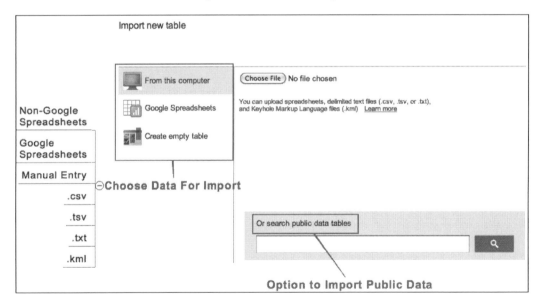

Search user community Fusion Tables at
http://www.google.com/fusiontables/search.

For the following example, the existing Spreadsheets file of Chicago Census 2010 data was imported into Fusion Tables. When Google Spreadsheets has been chosen as the imported source, any spreadsheets that exist in Google Drive will be available for import. In this instance, Chicago_Census_2010_Ages is selected and imported.

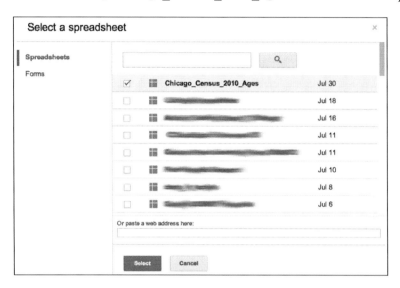

Once the import wizard has finished, the Fusion Tables file is given the default name, New Table. To change the filename as well as add additional attribute information to the Fusion Tables file, select **Edit** | **Modify Table Info** (or **File** | **Rename** in the experimental Fusion Tables version). In the pop-up window that appears, enter the desired table name as well as additional information about the data being used. For example, if the data was pulled from a website, it is appropriate to cite the website in the **Attribution page link** and/or **Description** fields. If a link is provided and the **Attribute data to** field is filled in, Fusion Tables will provide a clickable link under the filename to the link provided in Table Info.

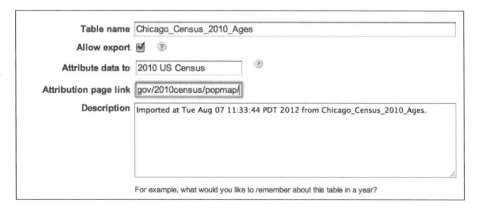

Data management

The **Edit** and **Merge** tabs are the key menu items for data management and manipulation. The **View** menu item holds options for creating data filters as well as viewing comments made on the various cell elements. Filters can also be applied by clicking on the **options** link just below the menu bar. The **Experiment** menu option is where newly released functions, specifically new visualization types, will reside. Finally, the publishing and sharing capabilities in Fusion Tables are available by clicking on the **Get Link** and **Share** buttons.

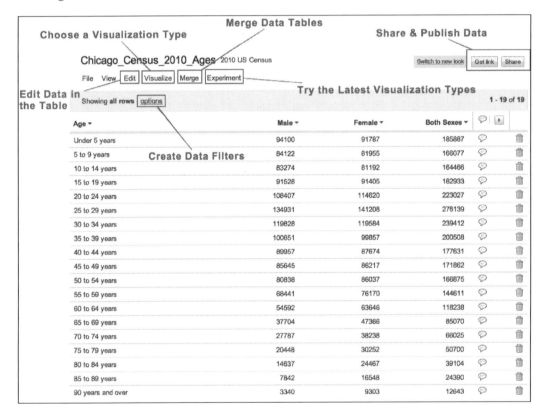

Editing rows

To modify cell content, click on the cell to edit. To add additional layout-conforming data to the table, select **Edit | Add row**. By selecting **Edit | Add Column** in the menu, an additional column is added to the table along with an additional visualization attribute.

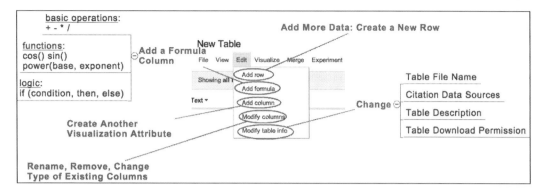

Modifying columns

Navigate to **Edit | Modify columns** to modify existing columns. This includes existing map attributes, including type, name, and order of appearance in the table. The following is the configuration used for the Fusion Tables maps example in this chapter:

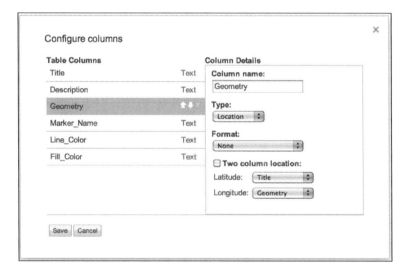

When configuring columns, it is often a good idea to delete all default columns completely before creating your own. Each Fusion Tables column is assigned a data type, causing pervasive formatting issues if a column is simply relabeled for another purpose. This is especially true for Location-type columns, as modifying a column from one type to another does not always translate correctly.

Adding a formula

When a mathematical or logical operation is to be performed on the table data, navigate to **Edit | Add Formula**. Configuring a formula automatically creates an additional column in the table, and thus can be used as an additional visualization attribute. The functions currently supported by the Fusion Tables formula option are as follows:

- Basic operations: +, -, *, and /

- Functions: `cos()`, `sin()`, and `power(base, exponent)`

- Logic: `if (condition, then, else)`

Views

Often times filtering a subset of data from the larger data set is desirable. This is a desirable feature to have when working with any data set that becomes too burdensome to view at once in its entirety. Select **File | Create View...** to select the columns to be included in the new view.

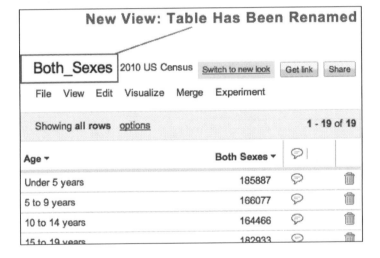

Setting up a view creates an entirely new Fusion Tables file in Google Drive. To switch between views, simply search or browse GDrive to find the desired views. As a best practice, creating a collection (folder) to contain the views is ideal. Also, creating meaningful titles for each view, and possibly referencing the original view in the filename are methods of best practice for organization.

New look in Fusion Tables

The new look in Fusion Tables is intended to support easier interface use and lessen the number of steps it takes to complete repetitive tasks when developing a visualization. These tasks mostly revolve around changing data settings and values and then visualizing them each time to view the result of the change. Row data editing remains similar to the view as presented by a spreadsheet. The Cards tabs present a preview of how data will look in an info window. The visualization of the data when using maps capabilities will appear in a third tab, and will be labeled the same as the location data column. Currently, at the time of publication, both the classic look and new look are available in Fusion Tables. However, new tables are created with the new look by default, and old tables have the option of either look.

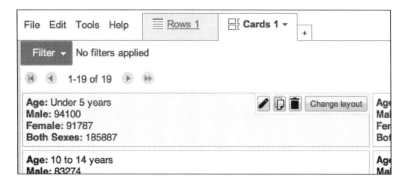

Merging tables

Fusion Tables provides basic table merge capabilities. Select **Merge | Table (File | Merge** in the newer experimental version). Follow the Merge with another table dialog to configure a table merge.

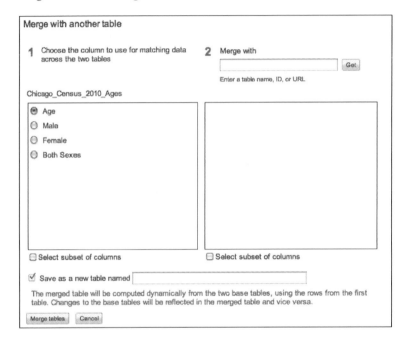

Creating a visualization

Select **Visualize | Line** to render the visualization of data. Visualization types compatible with the current data formatting will be available, while non-compatible formats will be grayed out.

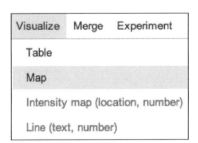

Non-map visualizations

Once **Visualize | Map** has been selected, Fusion Tables may require several configuration steps to properly graph the data. For example, Fusion Tables may ask the developer to select which row contains the column labels. Follow the online instructions to finish your particular visualization.

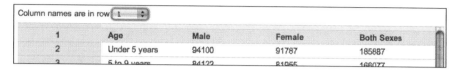

A simple line graph

The following graph was created by navigating to **Visualize | Line**. The graph is quite similar to the Spreadsheets version of the same chart. In the Fusion Tables version, additional filter controls are provided in the **options** link. Real-time filtering with the X Axis and Y Axis selection controls is also available. In the following graph, the filter controls are restricting the data viewed to only the number of males in each age group.

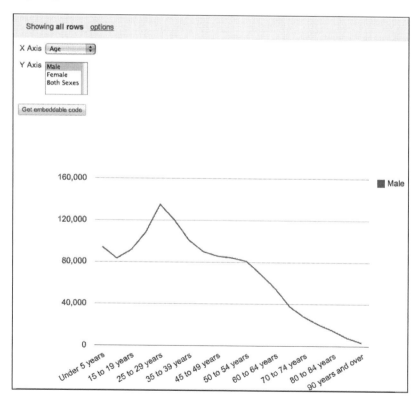

Experimental charts

Google is also actively developing new visualization types for Fusion Tables. The following visualization is the network graph type, found as an option under the **Experimental** tab at the time of publication. A network graph is used when it is helpful to view the relationships between data elements. For the Chicago 2010 Census data, relationships can be drawn between the age groups and number of persons in that particular age group. Network graphs also allow an additional element of weighting, based on a data attribute. In the following graph, the number of males in the age group is reflected as the size of the blue circles. Notice the young adult range 25 to 29 years. The circles are quite large. Then, look at the circle size for 90 years and over, which is quite small. The size difference of the circles indicates younger males are more in number than elderly males in Chicago during 2010. This conclusion corresponds with the previously presented line graph of the same data. The configuration of these filter elements can be changed dynamically using the drop-down and selection menus above the graph.

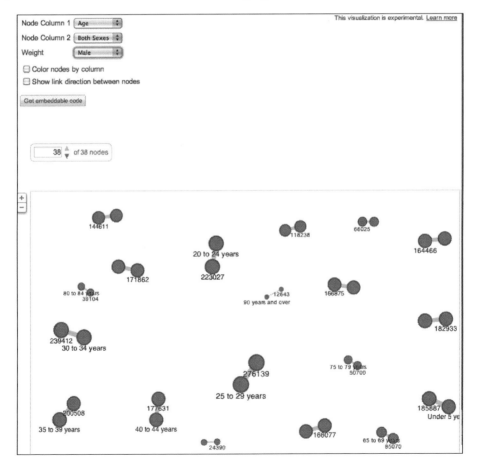

Mapping features

Customized, easy map creation is one of the core capabilities of Fusion Tables. One, or sometimes two columns are configured as the designated space where location information is stored. Mapping in general requires Geocoding, which is defined as any method that transforms human readable address information into latitude and longitude information. In Fusion Tables, the **Keyhole Markup Language** (**KML**) is used to extend geocoded data from a single point to multipoint lines and polygons. In Fusion Tables, a column is configured (using **Edit | Modify columns**) to accept data that is of the Location type. For the example discussed in the following section, the column that has been designated to hold location-type data is called Geometry.

 You can find more information about KML at `https://developers.google.com/kml/documentation/kml_tut`.

Geocoding

For this example, the primary method of setting points for markers, lines, and polygons is through latitude and longitude geocoding in a KML wrapper. The first topic to be covered is how to collect latitude and longitude information in the first place.

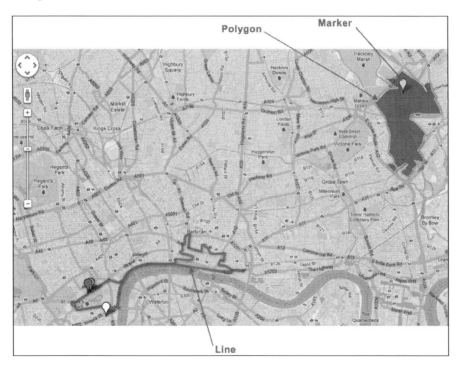

The following are data sources:

- **Marathon route map**: http://www.london2012.com/mm/Document/ Documents/General/01/25/71/49/OLYMarathoncourseGTW_Neutral.pdf
- **Olympic Park map**: http://www.london2012.com/mm/Document/ Documents/Venue/01/24/89/77/olympicparkmap2_Neutral.pdf
- **Westminster Abbey web page**: http://www.westminster-abbey.org/
- **Velodrome Information web page**: http://www.london2012.com/venue/ velodrome/

Manual method

Google Maps is a reliable method of manually collecting the geocoded information. Open Google Maps in a browser window. Zoom in on the location that is to be geocoded, and then pressing *Shift* right-click to bring up a pop-up window. In the pop-up window, select **What's here?**.

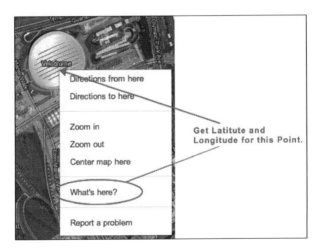

The **What's here?** selection will populate the Google search cell with the latitude and longitude of the point selected on the map. Copy and paste these coordinates into the **Location (Geometry)** column in Fusion Tables.

Address method

Fusion Tables itself is capable of providing a basic level of geocoding capability. Enter an address, including city, state, and zip code into a Geometry cell. Select **File | Geocode** to create a marker at that location on a map.

Then select **Visualize | Map** (select the **Geometry** tab in new look Fusion Tables version) to view the newly geocoded point on the map.

Google also provides an API to access Google geocoding capabilities, which is part of the Google Maps API Web Services collection. Fusion Tables limits geocoding to address, but the Geocoding API is capable of returning not only latitude and longitude, but also a variety of characteristics about the address.

You can find more information about Google Maps API Web Services Geocoding at `https://developers.google.com/maps/documentation/geocoding/`.

Third-party tools method

There are also tools generally available on the Internet to help with the task of geocoding. A free and easy-to-use tool is the EZ Google Maps Digitizer. Select a drawing mode or enter a location in the open field (the default is set to Mountain View, CA). The Polyline mode will capture a continuous series of mouse clicks on the map and render them as a line on the map. The Polygon mode collects a series of clicks on the map and renders them as a polygon. To transfer the geocoded points to Fusion Tables, copy and paste the coordinates into the appropriate cell, which is usually the **Geometry** column. The geocoding tool also inserts formatting into the code output, which should be reduced to only the necessary KML tags before visualizing.

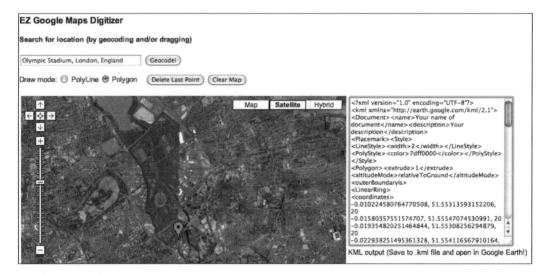

 You can find more information about EZ Google Maps Digitizer at `http://gmaps-samples.googlecode.com/svn/trunk/ ezdigitizer.htm`.

Recognizing errors

Geocoding and KML issues appear highlighted in yellow. If the formatting passes the Fusion Tables validity check, the language type appears by name and is followed by three periods. KML is generally the language used. In the following table excerpt, input in rows 1 and 2 have not been entered, resulting in small warning indicators in the fields.

The following screenshot shows incorrectly formatted input. The cell is missing the second of two geocoding latitude/longitude numbers, resulting in the cell value being highlighted.

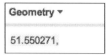

Once highlighted warnings have been resolved, testing geocoding accuracy is a good idea before visualizing the entire table. To test that a geocoded location appears as expected, hover over the **Geometry** column and a Google Earth; the marble-esque icon will appear in the far right of the cell. Select this Globe icon to preview the geocoded location on a map. If the marker appears where it is expected (and not in the middle of the ocean or something similar), the mapped location is correctly geocoded. If the point appears in the ocean or somewhere undesired, first swap the latitude and longitude points and re-test the preview. Also note that occasionally some points will pass the geocode preview test but still fail to appear on a map. Another potential issue involves incorrect formatting of a field, specifically KML tags. It's also possible that a style has been set incorrectly in Fusion Tables. Usually, verifying the correct formatting and geocoding solves most problems, with chart styles being an area to check as well.

Cell formatting

In Fusion Tables, the table cells can hold various types of map information when the content is formatted correctly. This includes some HTML tags, marker references, and HTML hexadecimal colors.

Markers, lines, and area

The Google Maps API, as well as built-in API functionality in Fusion Tables, has multiple ways to denote locations and areas on a map. **Markers** identify a single point on a map and often are represented by indicators of various colors, shapes, sizes, and graphics. They only require the latitude and longitude in the geocoding column. Marker icons available for public use are available from Google. They are referenced in Fusion Tables by using the name given to them on the following website.

 You can find more information about marker icons for use with Fusion Tables at `https://www.google.com/fusiontables/DataSource?snapid=99003`.

Lines are a series of points linked together using the KML tags `<lineString>` and `<coordinates>`. The structure of a KML entry in Fusion Tables is as follows:

```
<lineString><coordinates>
Coordinate Pair, 0
Coordinate Pair, 0
Coordinate Pair, 0
    .
    .
</coordinates></lineString>
```

A **polygon** is the mapping method used to outline an area on a map. The polygon is created by combining multiple latitude and longitude points, and then using KML tags to connect and shade the shape. The KML tags used for creating a polygon are `<Polygon>`, `<outerBoundaryIs>`, `<LinearRing>`, and `<coordinates>`. The structure of a polygon KML entry in the Fusion Tables **Geometry** column is as follows:

```
<Polygon><outerBoundaryIs><LinearRing><coordinates>
Coordinate Pair, 20
Coordinate Pair, 20
Coordinate Pair, 20
Coordinate Pair, 20
    .
    .
</coordinates></LinearRing></outerBoundaryIs><Polygon>
```

While previously mentioned as a potential pitfall when visualizing maps, map styles allow a developer to add dimensions and meaning to a map programmatically. Markers (points), polygons, and lines can be formatted to display various colors, transparencies, and sizes. Click on the **Configure styles** link after selecting **Visualize | Map** (**Tools | Change map styles...** in the new look Fusion Tables version, when location tab is selected) to open the **Change map styles** window. The **Fixed** and **Column** tabs allow a table column to set color or marker icon designation. The **Buckets** tab allows colors to be assigned to various data values. The **Gradient** tab is similar to the **Buckets** tab, but instead allows gradients of a single color to be assigned to groups of data values.

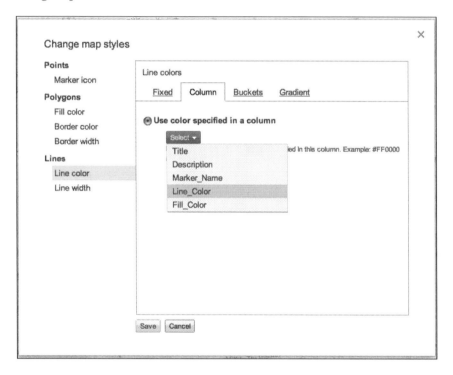

Info windows

Info windows are the pop-up windows that appear when an area or marker is clicked on a map. They usually contain various points of interest about the marked item on the map. The basic format for creating an info window is through HTML encapsulated in a cell on the Fusion Table, although the default is to display all columns for the entry, though not always desirable.

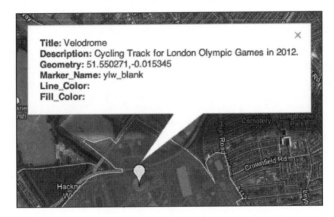

The info window layout can be automatically configured, or it can be configured with some customizations available by selecting which columns data to display in the window via **Change info window layout**. Launch the info window layout window by clicking on the **Configure info window** link under **Visualize | Map mode** (**Tools | Change info window layout...** in the new look Fusion Tables version). The **Automatic** tab allows for minimal modification, only allowing to select columns to be included or excluded. For a more customized info window, select the **Custom** link to edit the code directly.

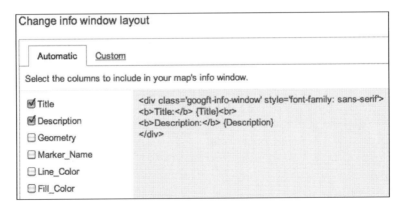

The following is an example of a maps window that has been modified from the default Fusion Tables settings. In the following code, the {Title} and {Description} tags are used to include the corresponding table columns in the window. The HTML div tags are used to format the window.

```
<div class='googft-info-window' style='font-family: sans-
serif'><b>{Title}</b><br>{description}</div>
```

Within the **Description** column, HTML is once again used to display a picture and create an active link to a website. The HTML used in the **Description** window is very simple, and mostly consists of the `<br>`, `<a href>`, and `<imgsrc=" >` tags.

 You can find a live example at https://www.google.com/
fusiontables/DataSource?docid=1NwzGHjDNiqGS7uFx
B5KB2lvnQ9wGr2ARHXjmq9g.

Summary

Spreadsheets charts and Fusion Tables are accessible entry points when starting to work with Google Visualizations. They provide insight and structure to fairly complex visualizations without requiring immense investment in learning API calls. While they do pose limitations in comparison to the API, Spreadsheets and Fusion Tables provide a simple method of creating visualizations, which can in turn be expanded by using Google API capabilities.

Note that advanced layering technique or view control customization is not part of the GUI Fusion Tables. Manipulating these advanced features, such as user defined search filters, unique styling of controls, and layer manipulation in the user interface must be developed using the Fusion Tables API, Maps API, and Visualization API. Data from Spreadsheets and particularly Fusion Tables is encouraged and these applications become primary data sources with bonus features that can only be unlocked through the API methods. Publishing options for the visualizations discussed in this chapter will be addressed in *Chapter 9, Publishing Options*.

In the next chapter, the creation of some basic visualizations shown as part of this chapter is discussed, but this time directly using the Visualization API.

4
Basic Charts

So far, the visualization examples in this book have relied heavily on the GUI interface of various Google applications. Unfortunately, the customization limitations of using only GUI applications quickly become evident. With the Google applications discussed in the previous chapters, Spreadsheets and Fusion Charts, it is fairly simple to create basic graphs and charts. Unfortunately, the sophistication of viewing controls, data source configuration, and even the style of the visualization itself is ultimately limited to the controls presented by default in the application. Apps Script gives some relief to the issue of customization, although limitations of the Apps Script platform impose their own set of limitations. Thus, what is needed is a customizable, feature-rich option, to build on top of the simplistic charts of Spreadsheets and Fusion Tables. The Google APIs, specifically the Visualization (Chart tools) API, are the required building blocks to accomplish this goal.

The world of Google APIs can at first appear somewhat overwhelming. However, the design and methodology behind all Google APIs is strikingly similar. This similarity exists because of an adherence by Google to standard programming elements, as well as existing JavaScript conventions. In addition, Google provides a methodic, nested approach to its API architecture.

Topics covered in this chapter:

- Crash-course in basic programming concepts
- Framework of the Visualization API
- A basic Chart: two methods

Visualization API Reference is available at `https://developers.google.com/chart/interactive/docs/reference`.

Programming concepts

This section presents a baseline of general programming concepts in an attempt to thwart the confusion of non-programmers while exploring the vast ocean of Google APIs. This brief introduction to programming is by no means a complete or authoritative source for the art that is application programming. Individuals often spend their lives learning the particularities of programming languages; others invest heavily in the improvement of the languages themselves. For the Google Visualization API, a more realistic approach is to provide universal concepts that are inherent in the Google API to developers that have little to no application programming experience. Readers with programming experience may wish to skip this section and go to the *Visualization API common Framework* section of this chapter.

Variables

Variables are locations in a program designated for storing information temporarily while an application runs. The application is able to access the variable and manipulate its contents. To illustrate, the task of a programming variable is somewhat similar to the aim of a mathematical equation variable. In an equation where $2 + x = 5$, the value assigned to the variable x for this instance would be 3. Also, it is worth noting that in this case the value of x will be static. Variables whose purpose is to not change is referred to as a **constant** variable.

The style used to set variables in Google API code follows this pattern:

```
varvariable_name = something
```

Here, the `variable_name` is a name chosen by the developer and should be representative of the something that's being stored in it.

Best practice

Use variable names that represent their purpose. For example: a variable name representing an `AreaChart` API function could be `ac`, which would be somewhat representative of the variable's purpose (AreaChart). Better yet, assigning a variable name of data for `DataTable` API function would be more representative. Note that, in general, variables x, y, z are not good representative variable names as it is easy to confuse their purposes in even a small amount of code.

In general, variables have the flexibility to assume various types. Text and numeric values are generic examples. With the Visualization API, the type of variable is automatically detected and generally does not require action on the part of the developer in order to set the correct type.

The various types of variables available in the Visualization API are as follows:

Number

In the programming world there are various types of numbers. In some programming languages, numbers need to be identified by type in the program in order for the program to recognize them properly. For example, the number 2 is an integer, but the number 2.222 is of a type called floating point due to its fraction in decimal format. However, for the general purpose of using the Visualization API, all types of numbers are treated simply as one type. In the previous example, 2 and 2.222 are both simply called numbers in the Visualization API.

Boolean

The concept of a Boolean value is fairly straightforward. A Boolean value can only hold the values "*True*" or "*False*". Using a Boolean variable is similar to asking a yes or no question without the ability to accept "maybe" as an answer. In programming practice, Boolean variables are very useful when a condition needs to be tested to be true or false before taking a certain action in the program. How to propose a condition to be tested is covered in the *Conditional logic* section of this chapter.

The Boolean method of logical decision-making was devised by the mathematician George Boole, and continues to bear his name.

String

A string is exactly as it sounds: it is a collection of *characters* saved in one variable. Note that characters are not simply A to Z and 0 to 9, but also include punctuation and often other special characters. Similar to number variables, strings can be used to hold information for the application, or store static information to be used by the application. For example, a string containing the characters that spell the word Google would look like this:

```
string_name = 'Google'
```

It is important that characters designated to be a single string must be enclosed in quotes. Depending on the specific program method being used, the quotes may be required to be single or double quotes. An example of using a string as a constant label is as follows:

```
Varname_label = 'Name: '
```

Here, `'Name: '` could be a field label appearing in an address form application. Note the blank space to the right of the colon. For strings, whitespace is considered a character and may change the expected output of an application if not taken into account.

Also, a variable may be used to store user input as a string. For example, to capture the name entered by a user in an address form application, a variable could be defined as follows:

```
Var name_field = ''
```

Notice, in the previous statement there is nothing, not even a whitespace, being stored in the `name_field` variable. When nothing is assigned to a variable, the variable is considered to have a value of **null**, or nothing. Giving a variable a value of null is commonly used to set a clean default state. When the application runs, the `name_field` variable can then be used with confidence to capture user input accurately. Given the variable name of `name_field`, it would seem that this particular variable is intended to capture name data from a form application.

Best practice

Remember that whitespace is a character if it is part of a string.

Array

Arrays look a lot like tables, but they are more versatile than a simple table as they can have various dimensions and hold several layers of information. Yet for purposes of the Visualization API, most arrays are generally two-dimensional, thus having the familiar format of columns and rows with single values in the cells. The underlying structure of the Visualization API `DataTable` function is essentially an array. The `DataTable` function is used to create a dataset within the API script. For example, the 2010 Chicago Census data from previous chapters can be created completely within the script, and then manipulated by the Visualization API. The following example constructs an array of data using a `DataTable` helper function called `arrayToDataTable()`, and consists of several lines of data from the 2010 Chicago Census data.

```
0   var data = google.visualization.arrayToDataTable([
1     ['Age',  'Male',  'Female',  'Both Sexes'],
2     ['Under 5 years',    94100,         91787,          185887],
3     ['5 to 9 years',     84122,         81955,          166077],
4     ['10 to 14 years',   83274,         81192,          164466],
5     ['15 to 19 years',   91528,         91405,          182933],
      ['20 to 24 years',  108407,        114620,          223027],

         0                 1              2                3

                             data[5,2]
```

To reference a specific cell in the data table, a coordinate system is used. For example, to find the number of females that are 20 to 24 years old, matrix coordinates are attached to the data variable.

```
data[5,2]
```

It is important to observe that the column and row ranges begin at zero and not with the number one. Also note the entries 'Under 5 years' is in quotes while the other entries are numbers. Arrays can hold a variety of data types; in this specific case, both strings and numbers are contained within a single array.

Equation

Just as in mathematics, **equations** in Google API applications are a method of performing an operation and equating it to something else. Common mathematical operators (+, -, *, /), as well as Boolean operators (*AND, OR, NOT*, or alternatively notated as &&, ||, !) can be used.

API call and attributes

Sometimes, when calling the Google APIs, it is helpful to save the resulting value. For example, if data is created or imported it is helpful to have a single name to reference the entire structure of data. Using the 2010 Census data for Chicago, a data array becomes encompassed in a variable through the use of the google.visualization.arrayToDataTable API call. Once the data variable is created, it can be referenced in the same code as an array data[x,y], or simply as data.

```
var data = google.visualization.arrayToDataTable([
    ['Age', 'Male', 'Female', 'Both Sexes'],
    ['Under 5 years',   94100,       91787,       185887],
    ['5 to 9 years',    84122,       81955,       166077]
]);
```

Conditional logic

The concept of conditional logic and loops is a natural continuation of the *Boolean* section discussed previously. Boolean logic is in fact the combination of *True* or *False* testing outcomes, also known as conditional logic. To create meaningful logic expressions, the Boolean operators *AND*, *OR*, and *NOT* are introduced. These operators are fairly self-explanatory in that they can be communicated as a sentence in regular language. For example, "If it is sunny *AND* warm, I will use my air conditioning".

The logical expression, written in pseudo syntax, to which the preceding sentence translates:

```
If (sunny AND warm) {
airconditioning = true
}
```

If statements, as seen previously, are to test for a condition. Sunny, as well as warm must be *true* in order for the preceding condition to be *true*. The testing result of *true* assigns air conditioning a value of *true*. This of course is an over simplification of the power of conditional logic, but does provide basic insight into the thought process. Additional tutorials on this topic can be found on the web.

Functions

Functions are essentially the "guts" of any application, and thus are also at the core of any application using the Google APIs. Rather than writing a program of unorganized components, functions are used to group snippets of code together by functionality. Conceptually, functions are the method a developer uses to create reusable tools. The following is the general structure of a function:

```
function doSomething () {
// create some variables...

//do some computation...

//return (or not) a result.

}
```

With the Visualization API, functions are the primary method of encapsulating all of the work that goes into creating the visualization itself.

Best practice
As with the variables, name functions should be named in such a way that the name is descriptive of the purpose they serve.

Classes (and objects)

Classes have the potential to be a confusing concept, but it also helps to remember the concept of classes in computer programming, which are no different than other areas of study. In biology, a class is part of a hierarchy that is used to define animals. In education, a class is a grouping of students whose learning progress is roughly of the same level (for example, 1st grade, 5th grade, and Kindergarten are all educational class groupings). Therefore, a class in computer programming is a set of instructions for building instances of functions. These instances, that can hold states, are called **Objects**. When using the Visualization API, requests to the API are formed in such a way as to reflect this hierarchy.

Libraries

In relation to the Visualization API, **Libraries** are a collection of classes that are used to build applications. Libraries generally consist of commonly used code, such as mathematical functions, that are needed regularly in most applications. Google has opted to call their API Libraries **packages**. For Google, API packages are the sets of Google objects that allow any programmer a path to manipulating Google's vast infrastructure.

Best practices
In addition to creating descriptive variable names, there are several additional programming habits that are considered best practice when writing code.

Commenting

The purpose of good commenting practice is to ensure that another developer will be able to determine the purpose of the application without significant forensic efforts. In general, single-line comments are marked by a double forward slash // and blocks of comments are indicated by a forward slash *plus* asterisks combination /*...*/. It is generally appropriate to provide a block comment at the beginning of a script, application, or even a function. There are a handful of topics that can be included in the comment block:

- Description of the overall functionality
- Name/contact information of the author
- Date of the last update
- Packages/libraries used
- Revision number

```
/* Description: This application draws a bar chart of some data.
Author: Traci Ruthkoski
Date Revised: 9/1/2012
*/
```

The purpose of single-line commenting is to give short descriptions of a specific line or section of code in order to aid in its readability. However, a potential pitfall when commenting is the overuse of comments, ultimately reducing the readability of the code.

```
var year='2012';   // Define the year.
```

Of course, lack of comments does not prevent code from running. The developer must determine the types of comments that are appropriate to their code. Ultimately, commenting is not a requirement but a strongly suggested element of an application, and is often a requirement when publishing applications to Google galleries and forums.

Spacing/format

When writing good code, it is also important to address its readability from a formatting perspective. Just as writing prose requires paragraphs and margins to be read easily, code is more readable when its logical functions are visually segmented. The collection of proper spacing and formatting for a given code language is known as **code conventions**. The following illustrates a simple framework for detecting an error in an application. Indentation indicates that the error checking statement is encapsulated within the computation of the DrawChart function.

```
function DrawChart {
    if (something == error) {
        message = 'This app encountered an error!'
    }
}
```

Visualization API common Framework

As discussed in *Chapter 2*, *Anatomy of a Visualization*, Visualization API code is JavaScript-based and resides within HTML <script> tags. Unless otherwise noted, it is assumed that all the API code intended for a HTML framework is located within these tags.

Load API modules

For all Google API code, including the Visualization API, there are several general components required. These are:

- Declaration of an API source URL
- Request API objects using the Google Loader

Inside the first `script` tag, a few short lines of HTML indicate the location of the Google Visualization API library, hosted by Google. The second `script` tag invokes a call to `google.load`, which is the Google Loader. The Google Loader options indicate which API is to be loaded for the application, as well as what packages and options for the API should also be loaded. The `google.load` call in the following sample script indicates that Version 1 of the Visualization API is to be loaded. It also indicates that the core chart package from the Visualization API module is to be retrieved. The Google Loader is a common component across all Google APIs, and is generally found shortly after the JavaScript declarations and source information.

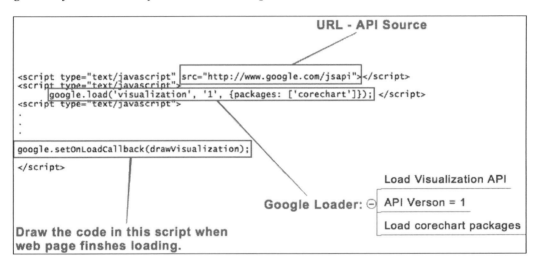

After the API source has been set and the API has been specified, the subsequent `script` tag set holds the actual API application logic. At the very end of the code, a final common component renders the visualization. The `google.setOn LoadCallback(drawVisualization);` line tells the Google Loader to execute `drawVisualization` once the page has loaded.

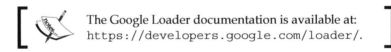

The Google Loader documentation is available at:
`https://developers.google.com/loader/`.

The combination of Visualization API packages and chart types is not particularly intuitive. The `corechart` package happens to contain the most types of chart. This is useful knowledge as visualizations that fall under the same package are most likely to be interchangeable, while other types almost certainly require a different data layout. At the time of publication, the following chart is a listing of current packages and chart types pairings. Note that older, depreciated versions of the API may still be available, but are instead covered under a Google depreciation policy.

Package	Chart type	Visual example
corechart	AreaChart	
corechart	BarChart	
corechart	BubbleChart	
corechart	CandlestickChart	
corechart	ColumnChart	

Package	Chart type	Visual example
corechart	ComboChart	
corechart	LineChart	
corechart	PieChart	
corechart	ScatterChart	

Package	Chart type	Visual example
`corechart`	`SteppedAreaChart`	
`imagechart`	`ImageChart` Depreciated, but available until April 20, 2015	
`imagechart`	`ImageCandlestickChart` Depreciated, but available until April 20, 2015	
`imagechart`	`ImageBarChart` Depreciated, but available until April 20, 2015	

Package	Chart type	Visual example
imageareachart	ImageAreaChart Depreciated, but available until April 20, 2015	
imagelinechart	ImageLineChart Depreciated, but available until April 20, 2015	
imagepiechart	ImagePieChart Depreciated, but available until April 20, 2015	
annotatedtimeline	AnnotatedTimeLine	

Package	Chart type	Visual example
charteditor	ChartEditor	
gauge	Gauge	
geochart	GeoChart	
geomap	GeoMap	
intensitymap	IntensityMap	
motionchart	MotionChart	

Package	Chart type	Visual example
orgchart	OrgChart	
imagesparkline	ImageSparkLine Depreciated, but available until April 20, 2015	
table	Table	
treemap	TreeMap	

> The preceding images can be found at `http://code.google.com/apis/ajax/playground/`.

Apps Script Wrapper

Just as HTML requires information regarding the location of the API objects, Apps Script requires its own wrapper to encapsulate API code. Depending on the integration with other Google Apps or as a stand-alone entity, the Apps Script wrapper can take several similar yet slightly different forms.

For Google Apps integration, especially with Google Spreadsheets, additional functionality in the GUI is often required. A typical need is an additional drop-down menu item from which the visualization of data is launched. To create a custom menu item in Google Spreadsheets, the Google UI (user interface) service must be used.

Using the Google UI service in Apps Script allows for building a user display, control interface, or an information capture method. The following image illustrates a realization of a custom menu item in the Spreadsheet menu bar.

To create the custom **Script Menu** item, the following function must be included in the Apps Script attached to the desired Google Spreadsheet file:

```
functiononOpen() {
   /* Retrieves the active spreadsheet as a source */
   var sheet = SpreadsheetApp.getActiveSpreadsheet();

   /* Create the menu entry for a function */
   var entries = [{

   /* Name of the dropdown list item */
   name : "Launch App",

functionName : "doGet"
}];
   /* Create the Spreadsheet Menu tab named "Script Menu" */
sheet.addMenu("Script Menu", entries);

};
```

Another common need is to have the resulting visualization display as a web page. In Apps Script, the designated function name doGet must be used in order to display the visualization on a web page. This is a specific requirement for the doGet function, is tied to Apps Script method of handling requests, and is a special, reserved function. Finally, if the visualization is to be rendered as a web page but as a standalone script in Google Drive, the two lines containing reference to the Spreadsheet application can be removed.

```
functiondoGet() {
   .
```

```
.
.
    // Use the UI service to create a UI for the app
    var ui = UiApp.createApplication();
    ui.add(chart);
    // Retreive information from the open spreadsheet
    var spreadsheet = SpreadsheetApp.getActiveSpreadsheet();
    // Show the UI in the spreadsheet application
    spreadsheet.show(ui);
}
```

or,

```
Var ui = UiApp.createApplication();
// No spreadsheet app here so show UI as a web app
ui.add(chart);
```

> Apps Script Ui Service documentation is available at
> `https://developers.google.com/apps-script/uiapp`.
> Information on displaying a User Interface from a Spreadsheet is
> available at `https://developers.google.com/apps-script/uiapp#DisplayingSpreadsheet`.

A basic visualization

With the general structure of visualization application established for both HTML-based and App Script apps, data and rendering code can now be added. For now, the data used in each sample is created within the script for purposes of illustration. In *Chapter 6, Data Manipulation and Sources*, data source connectivity outside the API script will be addressed. However, the following high-level logic for creating a visualization remains the same.

Logical steps to create a visualization are as follows:

1. Create/import/connect to the data.

2. Set the parameters, and perform calculations.

3. Render the Chart.

For the majority of developers, the most recognizable method of development is in a HTML context. For HTML, the Google Code Playground is perhaps the best development platform for newcomers.

Code Playground

Using the Google Code Playground, the following code renders the 2010 Chicago Census data used in the previous chapter examples.

```
function drawVisualization() {
  // Create and populate the data table.
  var data = google.visualization.arrayToDataTable([
    ['Age', 'Male', 'Female', 'Both Sexes'],
    ['Under 5 years',      94100,      91787,      185887],
    ['5 to 9 years',       84122,      81955,      166077],
    ['10 to 14 years',     83274,      81192,      164466],
    ['15 to 19 years',     91528,      91405,      182933],
    ['20 to 24 years',    108407,     114620,      223027],
    ['25 to 29 years',    134931,     141208,      276139],
    ['30 to 34 years',    119828,     119584,      239412],
    ['35 to 39 years',    100651,      99857,      200508],
    ['40 to 44 years',     89957,      87674,      177631],
    ['45 to 49 years',     85645,      86217,      171862],
    ['50 to 54 years',     80838,      86037,      166875],
    ['55 to 59 years',     68441,      76170,      144611],
    ['60 to 64 years',     54592,      63646,      118238],
    ['65 to 69 years',     37704,      47366,       85070],
    ['70 to 74 years',     27787,      38238,       66025],
    ['75 to 79 years',     20448,      30252,       50700],
    ['80 to 84 years',     14637,      24467,       39104],
    ['85 to 89 years',      7842,      16548,       24390],
    ['90 years and over',3340,         9303,        12643]
  ]);

  // Create and draw the visualization.
  new google.visualization.AreaChart(document.getElementById('visuali
zation')).
      draw(data, {curveType: "function",
               width: 600, height: 400,
               vAxis: {title: 'Population'},
               hAxis: {title: 'Age Groups'}


      );

}
```

First, in the `drawVisualization` function, a data variable is created to house the census data. Next, the data variable is passed to the `chart.draw()` method and is rendered via the API. With the call to draw the visualization, additional formatting parameters are included at the same time.

Finally, in its HTML form entirety, the Area Chart visualization of the 2010 Chicago Census data looks like the following code:

```
<!--
You are free to copy and use this sample in accordance with the terms
of the
Apache license (http://www.apache.org/licenses/LICENSE-2.0.html)
-->

<!DOCTYPE html PUBLIC "-//W3C//DTD XHTML 1.0 Strict//EN" "http://www.
w3.org/TR/xhtml1/DTD/xhtml1-strict.dtd">
<html xmlns="http://www.w3.org/1999/xhtml">
  <head>
    <meta http-equiv="content-type" content="text/html;
charset=utf-8"/>
    <title>
      Google Visualization API Sample
    </title>
    <script type="text/javascript" src="http://www.google.com/
jsapi"></script>
    <script type="text/javascript">
      google.load('visualization', '1', {packages: ['corechart']});
    </script>
    <script type="text/javascript">
      function drawVisualization() {
        // Create and populate the data table.
        var data = google.visualization.arrayToDataTable([
          ['Age', 'Male', 'Female', 'Both Sexes'],
          ['Under 5 years',   94100,     91787,       185887],
          ['5 to 9 years',    84122,     81955,       166077],
```

```
            ['10 to 14 years',    83274,      81192,      164466],
            ['15 to 19 years',    91528,      91405,      182933],
            ['20 to 24 years',   108407,     114620,      223027],
            ['25 to 29 years',   134931,     141208,      276139],
            ['30 to 34 years',   119828,     119584,      239412],
            ['35 to 39 years',   100651,      99857,      200508],
            ['40 to 44 years',    89957,      87674,      177631],
            ['45 to 49 years',    85645,      86217,      171862],
            ['50 to 54 years',    80838,      86037,      166875],
            ['55 to 59 years',    68441,      76170,      144611],
            ['60 to 64 years',    54592,      63646,      118238],
            ['65 to 69 years',    37704,      47366,       85070],
            ['70 to 74 years',    27787,      38238,       66025],
            ['75 to 79 years',    20448,      30252,       50700],
            ['80 to 84 years',    14637,      24467,       39104],
            ['85 to 89 years',     7842,      16548,       24390],
            ['90 years and over',3340,         9303,       12643]
         ]);


         // Create and draw the visualization.
         new google.visualization.AreaChart(document.getElementById('vi
sualization')).
      draw(data, {curveType: "function",
        width: 600, height: 400,
        title:'Chicago Population by Age and Sex - 2010 Census',
        vAxis: {title: 'Population'},
        hAxis: {title: 'Age Groups'}
        }
      );
   }


      google.setOnLoadCallback(drawVisualization);
    </script>
  </head>
  <body style="font-family: Arial;border: 0 none;">
    <div id="visualization" style="width: 500px;
height: 400px;"></div>
  </body>
</html>
```

For additional `chart.draw()` configuration options using `AreaChart`, check the following link:

`https://developers.google.com/chart/interactive/docs/gallery/`
`areachart#Configuration_Options`

If the documentation style used by Google is unfamiliar, refer to the following image as an aid.

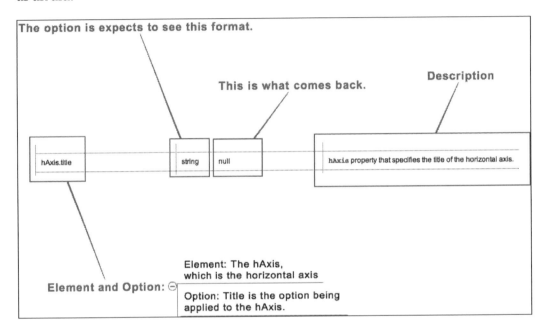

The Visualization API and Google APIs in general follow the preceding documentation convention.

> For experienced JavaScript users, `Chart.draw()` options follow standard JavaScript object literal syntax.

Apps Script

For an Apps Script visualization of the same 2010 Census data, similar but equivalent API calls are used to create a data variable and then render the data as an area chart.

```
functiondoGet() {

var data = Charts.newDataTable()
  .addColumn(Charts.ColumnType.STRING, "Age")
```

```
    .addColumn(Charts.ColumnType.NUMBER,  "Male")
    .addColumn(Charts.ColumnType.NUMBER,  "Female")
    .addColumn(Charts.ColumnType.NUMBER,  "Both Sexes")
    .addRow(['Under 5 years',      94100,    91787,    185887])
    .addRow(['5 to 9 years',       84122,    81955,    166077])
    .addRow(['10 to 14 years',     83274,    81192,    164466])
    .addRow(['15 to 19 years',     91528,    91405,    182933])
    .addRow(['20 to 24 years',     108407,   114620,   223027])
    .addRow(['25 to 29 years',     134931,   141208,   276139])
    .addRow(['30 to 34 years',     119828,   119584,   239412])
    .addRow(['35 to 39 years',     100651,   99857,    200508])
    .addRow(['40 to 44 years',     89957,    87674,    177631])
    .addRow(['45 to 49 years',     85645,    86217,    171862])
    .addRow(['50 to 54 years',     80838,    86037,    166875])
    .addRow(['55 to 59 years',     68441,    76170,    144611])
    .addRow(['60 to 64 years',     54592,    63646     118238])
    .addRow(['65 to 69 years',     37704,    47366,    85070])
    .addRow(['70 to 74 years',     27787,    38238,    66025])
    .addRow(['75 to 79 years',     20448,    30252,    50700])
    .addRow(['80 to 84 years',     14637,    24467,    39104])
    .addRow(['85 to 89 years',     7842,     16548,    24390])
    .addRow(['90 years and over', 3340,     9303,     12643])
    .build();


var chart = Charts.newAreaChart()
    .setDataTable(data)
    .setDimensions(600, 400)
    .setXAxisTitle("Age Groups")
    .setYAxisTitle("Population")
    .setTitle("Chicago Population by Age and Sex - 2010 Census")
    .build();

varui = UiApp.createApplication();
ui.add(chart);
returnui;
}
```

The purpose of illustrating equivalent methods through both the HTML and
Apps Script example is to demonstrate that there is no single method of coding
a visualization. Instead, there are multiple options available. Choosing an option
becomes dependent on the overall application purpose.

Summary

In general, learning the structure of the Google API environment is just as valuable as viewing specific examples of code. With the knowledge of how an API application fits within other Google Applications and also HTML, a developer is able to capitalize on the integrated nature of Google products. Furthermore, familiarity with the general Google API structure benefits not only Visualization API application work, but also any other Google API use.

This chapter presented the basic information required to code a simple visualization with the Google API, in particular the Visualization API. Limitations of chart creation that have not yet been addressed are more eloquent data retrieval, interactive abilities, and customized formatting of the charts themselves. So far, relatively little code has been required to create visualizations presentations. This trend continues as the style formatting issue is addressed in the next chapter.

5
Formatting Charts

Customization of visualization colors, fonts, views, and other visual attributes add readability and meaning to data displays. In both Spreadsheets and Fusion Tables, the Chart Editor is available in a GUI format, allowing non-programmers to set style choices. The Visualization API presents a larger set of customization options, including style options available through GUI methods. API-based style options include color and font styling, but also include the ability to graphically represent changes in data values through animated transitions. Finally, any style options configured through the Chart Editor in Spreadsheets or Fusion Tables can be set by individual end users by embedding the API Chart Editor component within the visualization itself.

Topics covered in this chapter are as follows:

- Spreadsheets and Fusion Tables customization
    - ◦ Colors and fonts
    - ◦ Filters

- Visualization API
    - ◦ Colors, fonts, and labels
    - ◦ Axis options
    - ◦ DataTable formatters

- Animated transitions
- Chart Editor

Regardless of the method used, style options can largely be divided into categories based on the nature of user interaction when viewing the final chart. These style categories are both static and dynamic/interactive.

Static

Static style options are those that are generally not intended for end-user interaction. Fonts, axis labels, colors, and filters fall under the static category. However, many of these options can become interactive as user controls and dashboards are added to the chart.

Spreadsheets

Customizable formatting options for Spreadsheets can be found in the Chart Editor. Instructions on using the built-in Spreadsheets Chart Editor was discussed in *Chapter 3, Spreadsheets, Charts, and Fusion Tables*. Options to customize the look of the data table itself are found under the **Format** menu tab. Additionally, the **Conditional formatting...** option under the **Format** tab includes conditional logic options similar to those found in any basic spreadsheet application. (Example logic: Color the cell green if value is above 10.)

For Spreadsheets, non-API styling capability does not extend beyond basic spreadsheet logic and Chart Editor options. It is possible to use the Visualization API inside an Apps Script attached to a spreadsheet, but this option is an extension of Spreadsheets and not considered built-in as it is not a GUI capability.

Fusion Tables

Through data filters and views, Fusion Tables offers a slightly more robust formatting option than Spreadsheets. For font and color styling, the Chart Editor is used. Fusion Tables Chart Editor in fact is the same underlying Chart Editor object that also appears as a built-in function to Spreadsheets. Yet in Fusion Tables, the new look version of the application affords additional usability beyond just the Chart Editor. In the newer version, charts are created as tabs and can be kept as a collection. This arranging ability allows for a variety of filters, charts, and views of the same data set to be displayed in one location. Although still in transition at the time of publication, it is expected the new look for Fusion Tables will quickly become the default interface.

The following example is a pie chart created in Fusion Tables using the Chicago 2010 Census data. This chart is a visualization of the male population only, with the slices in hue color representing a subset of larger age groupings. According to the data, Chicago appears to be a young city, with a little over half of its male population under the age of 40 in 2010. Color formatting is a particularly useful added dimension to a chart. Due to this, in the following example, it can be easily determined that 75 percent of the Chicago male population is under 50 years of age, given how the blue and green hues visually represent this population segment.

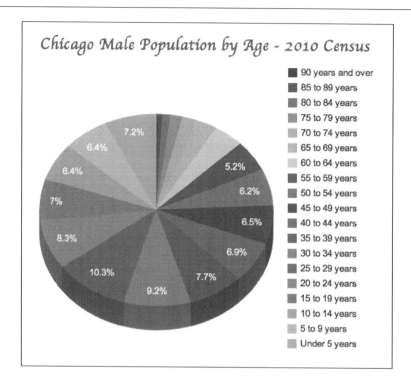

When creating a chart in Fusion tables, it is possible that by default the chart settings may or may not match the expected display for the particular visualization. For example, in order for all segments to be displayed, the preceding pie chart required the slice count to be set from the default to 19, which is the number of age categories in the data set.

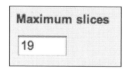

Best practice tip

It is always worthwhile to double-check the constraints of the chart type in order to be sure all desired data is accounted for in the graphic.

Chart Editor

To alter the style settings of a visualization in Fusion Tables (New Look), click on the **Change appearance...** button in the top-right corner of the chart.

In Fusion Tables, the **Change appearance...** button is simply an instance of the Chart Editor, with functions described in *Chapter 3, Spreadsheets, Charts, and Fusion Tables*.

Filters

To create a visualization of a subset of data, Fusion Tables is capable of creating filters. Select the blue **Filter** drop-down button in the top-left corner of the chart. The drop-down menu will contain the options for the data which can be filtered and displayed. Options available should match the columns in the table. In the following screenshot, the male population of Chicago has been filtered to view only the male population under 50 years of age. It can be noted that the age distribution of the subgroup under 50 years of age is fairly evenly distributed, with the 25 to 29 age group being a few percentages higher than the rest.

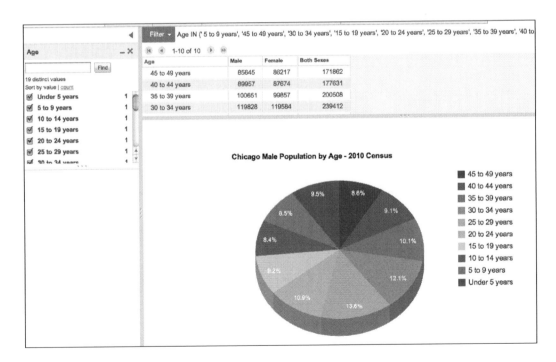

You can find the live example at `https://www.google.com/fusiontables/DataSource?docid=1Olo92KwNin8wB4PK_dBDS9eghe80_4kjMzOTSu0#chartnew:id=8`.

API

The Visualization API offers a significant number of options for style customization. Fine-grained control of color, font, size, and view are possible through the `chart.draw()` or `table.draw()` options, as well as through Cascading Style Sheet declaration methods. Special icon graphics are included in tables, in addition to the expected chart color and font styling. These special graphics are called **formatters** and are provided as an API function.

Colors and fonts: Inline

To provide the style flexibility when setting a table or chart color scheme, the `draw()` method is used. Both the table and chart draw calls require the data set variable and list of options to be set.

```
chart.draw(data_variable, options)
```

Or

```
table.draw(data_variable, options)
```

The list of options can be included directly in the `draw()` line of code, or passed to the call as a variable. The inline option for `draw()` follows this format:

```
table.draw(data, {option_name: value})
```

Where passing a list of options to the `draw()` method would be as follows:

```
var options = {
  width: 400,
  height: 240,
  title: 'Title of Graph',
  colors: ['#hex_color1', '#hex_color2', '#hex_color3'] };

chart.draw(data, options);
```

To include additional options in the list, simply use a comma between each option. Regarding option availability, the type of chart determines each chart's options. Documentation for option formatting can be found with the corresponding chart type documentation on the Google Chart Tools Developers web page.

You can find more information about Google Chart Developers at https://developers.google.com/chart/.

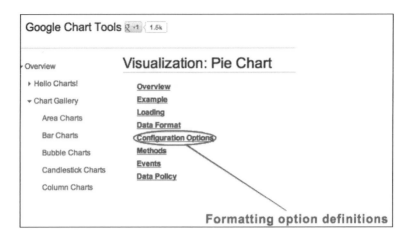

Finally, to recreate the pie chart of Chicago's 2010 male population shown earlier in this chapter using the API, the following formatting information would be used. Note the DataTable has been omitted, as it remains identical to previous examples but would be required for a complete recreation of the chart rendering.

```
new google.visualization.PieChart(document.getElementById('visualizat
ion')).
  draw(data, {

    title:"Chicago Male Population by Age - 2010 Census",
    titleTextStyle:
    {color: #635A5E, fontName: 'cursive', fontSize:  25},
    colors:
['#84160C', '#CC0000', '#E06666', '#E69138', '#F6B26B', '#F1C232',
'#FFD966', '#A64D79', '#C27BA0', '#674EA7', '#8E7CC3', '#3C78D8',
'#6D9EEB', '#3D85C6', '#6FA8DC', '#6AA84F', '#93C47D', '#B6D7A8',
'#A2C4C9'],

is3D:true,

reverseCategories:true

});
```

Colors and fonts: Cascading Style Sheets

Style options for a table can also be set using Cascading Style Sheets. The style definitions using CSS within the API script follow the same conventions as with HTML. The defined CSS styles are then grouped together by creating a variable that holds the information matching a CSS style to a specific table component.

```
<style type='text/css'>
  .table-color {
    color: #635A5E;
  }

  .big-font {
    font-size: 25px;
  }

  .header-font {
    font-style: cursive;
  }

</style>


  . . .


var cssClassNames = {
  'headerRow': 'big-font header-font',
  'tableRow': 'table-color'
  };

var options = {'cssClassNames': cssClassNames};
```

Finally, the `table.draw()` call uses the `options` variable by effectively passing the CSS information along to the visualization `draw()` method.

 You can find a CSS example at `https://developers.google.com/chart/interactive/docs/examples`.

Note that it also follows that charts are theoretically able to inherit styles from CSS files given their adherence to framework standards, of course assuming the chart itself allows the configuration.

Views

Regardless of the size of a dataset, it may be desirable to only show a portion of the data in a particular chart. The Visualization API offers a method to create data-targeted charts by using the `DataView` class. Additionally, Data Views are nested and thus provide the ability to create views from other views. Through the `DataView` class, it is also possible to create different styles of horizontal and vertical axes.

Using DataView

`DataView` does not change data values, but instead designates which columns are to be viewed in the chart. It is also possible to specify particular rows as viewable. Both row and column views can be set manually by designating them directly in the view, or programmatically through other decision processes. The following example is a view intended to only show the age group categories and corresponding population numbers for males from the 2010 Chicago Census data. The code for creating and drawing the view itself is included here, but note in the live example the data in `DataTable` does not change in order to create the view.

```
// Make a view of only age groups and males
var dataView = new google.visualization.DataView(data);
dataView.setColumns([0,1]);
// Draw a table with the new view
var table = new google.visualization.Table(document.
getElementById('table'));
table.draw(dataView, {width: 400, height: 200});
// Draw a chart with the new view
var chart = new google.visualization.ColumnChart(document.
getElementById('chart'));
chart.draw(dataView, {width: 400, height: 200});
```

Here we designated the columns to be viewed by using the `setColumns` function of `DataView` and set the configuration to a variable. Next, the new variable containing the view information is used to create a chart. In the preceding code snippet, the new view, `dataView`, is used to create a table in addition to a chart. The titles of the new view are defined as ordinary HTML. The resulting visualization is as follows:

Chicago Census by Age - 2010			
Age	**Male**	**Female**	**Both Sexes**
Under 5 years	94100	91787	185887
5 to 9 years	84122	81955	166077
10 to 14 years	83274	81192	164466
15 to 19 years	91528	91405	182933
20 to 24 years	108407	114620	223027
25 to 29 years	134931	141208	276139
30 to 34 years	119828	119584	239412
35 to 39 years	100651	99857	200508
40 to 44 years	89957	87674	177631

2010 Census by Age - Males Only

You can find a live example at `http://gvisapi-packt.` `appspot.com/ch5-examples/ch5-dataview.html`.

Axes options

For both horizontal and vertical chart axes, there are several basic customization options. Just as with other chart customizations, the axes are modified through the `chart.draw()` function. To modify the horizontal axis, the `hAxis` option of `chart.draw()` is used. Similarly, to format the vertical axis, `vAxis` of `chart.draw()` is implemented. For example, in order to set the horizontal axis title to "Age Groups" on the Census Area Chart, the following option would be listed in the `AreaChart.draw()` function:

```
hAxis: {title: 'Age Groups'}
```

To discuss advanced axis options, it is important to first understand several terms associated with axes. Firstly, axes can be defined as discrete or continuous. A discrete axis is one that has values that are defined into categories or groups. These groups are also evenly spaced. The Chicago Census data has a column of a series of age groups, which is interpreted as a discrete axis. A continuous axis has an infinite number of values. The population number axis of the Chicago Census is considered a type of continuous axis in this case, even though its values (population) are not truly infinite.

In addition to being either discrete or continuous, an axis can be either major or minor. A **major axis** is the natural interpretation of the chart. In the Chicago Census example, the age groups make up the major axis because the age groups are the intended primary focus relative to the population count. A **minor axis** is the secondary element in the graph, in this case being the population per age category. Finally, while the major axis is more likely to be the horizontal axis, this is not necessarily always the case. Other rules to know regarding major/minor and discrete/continuous axes are as follows:

- The major axis can be horizontal or vertical
- The major axis can be discrete or continuous
- The minor axis is always continuous

Most axis settings will conform to the type of chart and data represented. However, it is possible to control the type of major axis through the `dataView.SetColumns` attribute, which was previously used in this chapter to set views. To make an axis discrete, set the type to `string` inside the `dataView.SetColumns` attribute.

```
// Set column 1 to be string
dataView.SetColumns([1, type: 'string' ]);
```

To convert a discrete axis to continuous, set the type to `number`, `date`, `datetime`, or `timeofday`.

The Axes Options documentation is available at `https://developers.google.com/chart/interactive/docs/customizing_axes`.

DataTable formatters

Formatters are special functions provided by the API that insert graphic representations into a table visualization. There is a handful of formatters available:

- Arrow
- Bar
- Color
- Date
- Number
- Pattern

All formatters follow the same method as other API calls, with the formatter name followed by its options. The following line creates the formatter object:

```
google.visualization.formatter_name(options)
```

Formatters only affect one column at a time. To format multiple columns, use multiple formatter calls. The following line applies the formatter to the second column in the data table (first column is 0):

```
Formatter_name.format(data, 1);
```

In addition, formatters require that the `AllowHTML` option from `table.draw()` is set to `true`. This requirement is due to the fact that formatters are rendered as HTML, and thus HTML must be allowed in the table in order to be viewed properly.

In summary, the process for using a formatter is as follows:

1. Create the data table.
2. Create formatter(s).
3. Apply formatter(s) to a column(s).
4. Draw the table.

 Formatters can only be used with `DataTable` and not `DataView` as `DataView` is read-only.

Arrow

The arrow formatter creates arrow icons next to values in the table. The arrow is green and points upward when the value in the table cell is above a certain value. Similarly, the arrow is red and points downward when the cell value is below a certain threshold. If the value is equal to the threshold value, no arrow is displayed.

In the following example, the threshold value is set to 0, which is also the default.

To change the threshold value, use the `base` option available for `TableArrowFormat`. The following line sets the threshold for comparison to a value `12`.

```
var formatter = new google.visualization.TableArrowFormat({base: 12});
```

> A live example is available at http://gvisapi-packt.appspot.com/ch5-examples/ch5-arrowformatter.html.

Bar

The bar formatter creates a bar-shaped visualization of the value in an adjacent column in the table. Just as with arrow formatters, bar formatters are also able to receive options at the time the formatter object is created. In the following example, a bar formatter is created for the male, female, and total population columns of the Chicago Census 2010 data. A new formatter must be created for each column. The bar colors, size, and maximum value are set using the formatter options available through the API.

```
<!DOCTYPE html PUBLIC "-//W3C//DTD XHTML 1.0 Strict//EN"
"http://www.w3.org/TR/xhtml1/DTD/xhtml1-strict.dtd">
<html xmlns="http://www.w3.org/1999/xhtml">
<head>
  <meta http-equiv="content-type" content="text/html;
  charset=utf-8" />
  <title>Google Visualization API Sample</title>
  <script type="text/javascript"
  src="http://www.google.com/jsapi"></script>
  <script type="text/javascript">
    google.load('visualization', '1', {packages: ['table']});
    function drawVisualization() {
```

```
    // Create and populate the data table.
    var data = google.visualization.arrayToDataTable([
      ['Age', 'Male', 'Female', 'Both Sexes'],
      ['Under 5 years',      94100,      91787,      185887],
      ['5 to 9 years',       84122,      81955,      166077],
      ['10 to 14 years',     83274,      81192,      164466],
      ['15 to 19 years',     91528,      91405,      182933],
      ['20 to 24 years',     108407,     114620,     223027],
      ['25 to 29 years',     134931,     141208,     276139],
      ['30 to 34 years',     119828,     119584,     239412],
      ['35 to 39 years',     100651,     99857,      200508],
      ['40 to 44 years',     89957,      87674,      177631],
      ['45 to 49 years',     85645,      86217,      171862],
      ['50 to 54 years',     80838,      86037,      166875],
      ['55 to 59 years',     68441,      76170,      144611],
      ['60 to 64 years',     54592,      63646,      118238],
      ['65 to 69 years',     37704,      47366,      85070],
      ['70 to 74 years',     27787,      38238,      66025],
      ['75 to 79 years',     20448,      30252,      50700],
      ['80 to 84 years',     14637,      24467,      39104],
      ['85 to 89 years',     7842,       16548,      24390],
      ['90 years and over', 3340,        9303,       12643]
    ]);

// Create and draw the visualization.
var table = new
google.visualization.Table(document.getElementById
('visualization'));

// Create formatters for each column
var formatter_male = new
google.visualization.TableBarFormat({width: 200,
colorPositive: 'blue', max: 276139});

var formatter_female = new
google.visualization.TableBarFormat({width: 200,
colorPositive: 'blue', max: 276139});

var formatter_both = new
google.visualization.TableBarFormat({width: 200,
colorPositive: 'green', max: 276139});

// Apply formatter to male, female, & both sexes columns
  formatter_male.format(data, 1);
```

```
        formatter_female.format(data, 2);
        formatter_both.format(data, 3);

        table.draw(data, {allowHtml: true,
        alternatingRowStyle: true});
    }

    google.setOnLoadCallback(drawVisualization);
  </script>
</head>
<body style="font-family: Arial;border: 0 none;">
<div id="visualization" style="width: 1200px; height: 500px;"></div>
</body>
</html>
```

The following is the resulting visualization from the preceding example code:

Age	Male	Female	Both Sexes
Under 5 years	94100	91787	185887
5 to 9 years	84122	81955	166077
10 to 14 years	83274	81192	164466
15 to 19 years	91528	91405	182933
20 to 24 years	108407	114620	223027
25 to 29 years	134931	141208	276139
30 to 34 years	119628	119584	239412
35 to 39 years	100651	99857	200508
40 to 44 years	89957	87674	177631
45 to 49 years	85645	86217	171862
50 to 54 years	80838	86037	166875
55 to 59 years	68441	76170	144611
60 to 64 years	54592	63646	118238
65 to 69 years	37704	47366	85070
70 to 74 years	27787	38238	66025
75 to 79 years	20448	30252	50700
80 to 84 years	14637	24467	39104
85 to 89 years	7842	16548	24390
90 years and over	3340	9303	12643

A live example is available at `http://gvisapi-packt.appspot.com/ch5-examples/ch5-barformatter.html`.

Color

The color formatter allows the developer to programmatically set color values for cells in a table visualization. Similar to the capabilities of general spreadsheet applications, cells can also be set to vary in color depending on an assigned mathematical condition. For example, in the following snippet of a table containing the Chicago Census 2010 data, the color of the cell is red with a white font if the number of individuals in that particular group is between 0 and 10000. The same cell is formatted orange with a white font if the number of individuals is between 10001 and 99999.

70 to 74 years	27787	38238	66025
75 to 79 years	20448	30252	50700
80 to 84 years	14637	24467	39104
85 to 89 years	7842	16548	24390
90 years and over	3340	9303	12643

 A live example is available at `http://gvisapi-packt.appspot.com/ch5-examples/ch5-colorformatter.html`.

Date

To display a date in a table, use the `DateFormat` formatter. The `DateFormat` Formatter has three options: `short`, `medium`, and `long`. The format option type is set at the time of the creation of the formatter.

```
var formatter = new google.visualization.DateFormat({formatType:'medi
um'});
```

The `short`, `medium`, and `long` types refer to the style in which the date is displayed. The `short` format is represented only with numbers and the year is truncated to two digits. The `medium` format uses all four digits of the year and provides the name of the month in its abbreviated form. The `long` format is the same as the `medium` format, but the name of the month is spelled out in its entirety.

Census Year	Date Taken (Short)	Date Taken (Medium)	Date Taken (Long)
1990	4/1/90	Apr 1, 1990	April 1, 1990
2000	4/1/00	Apr 1, 2000	April 1, 2000
2010	4/1/10	Apr 1, 2010	April 1, 2010

 A live example is available at `http://gvisapi-packt.appspot.com/ch5-examples/ch5-dateformatter.html`.

Number

To indicate special formatting for numbers, the number formatter is used. In the following example, the font color is set based on a positive or negative numerical value.

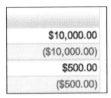

The number formatter can also be set to indicate a prefix or suffix symbol and provide parentheses for negative values. Formatting is set in a similar manner to other formatters using the `options` method.

```
var formatter =
new google.visualization.TableNumberFormat(
    {prefix: "$", negativeColor: 'red', negativeParens: true});
```

 A live example is available at http://gvisapi-packt.appspot. com/ch5-examples/ch5-numberformatter.html.

Pattern

The purpose of a pattern formatter is to condense two columns of information into a single column for display. This method is particularly useful when creating a table of URL links or mailto links. To create a table with a pattern formatter, select two columns to condense as a display. In the following example, the website name's column and corresponding URL's column are condensed to produce a live link for each site.

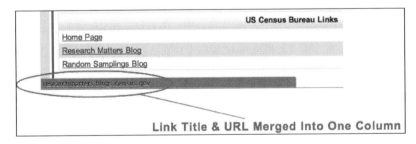

The previous sample was created from the following code:

```
// Create and populate the data table.
var data = google.visualization.arrayToDataTable([
    ['US Census Bureau Links', 'URL'],
    ['Home Page', 'www.census.gov/'],
    ['Research Matters Blog',
    'researchmatters.blogs.census.gov'],
    ['Random Samplings Blog', 'blogs.census.gov'],
    ]);

// Create and draw the visualization.
var table = new google.visualization.Table(document.getElementById('vi
sualization'));

var formatter = new google.visualization.TablePatternFormat('<a
href="http://{1}">{0}</a>');

formatter.format(data, [0, 1]); // Apply formatter and set the
formatted value of the first column.

var view = new google.visualization.DataView(data);

view.setColumns([0]); // Create a view with the first column only.
table.draw(view, {allowHtml: true});
```

> A live example is available at `http://gvisapi-packt.appspot.`
> `com/ch5-examples/ch5-pattern.html`.
>
> You can find more information about Formatter Documentation at
> `https://developers.google.com/chart/interactive/docs/`
> `reference#formatters`.

Paging

Formatting a table into pages is a common practice when a long list of data needs to be presented in a small amount of space. The `DataTable` object allows for the enabling and customization of paging on table renderings. To convert a basic table into a paged table, add the following option to the `table.draw()` call.

```
page: true
```

Paging configurations may also be further customized. The full API request with the option to restrict the number of items per page to 5 is as follows:

```
table.draw(data, {allowHtml: true, page: 'enable', pageSize: 5});
```

Additional format settings can also be included in the options list, including how many rows to display per page (pageSize), the page to display by default (startPage), and paging icons or text to replace the default arrow buttons (pagingSymbols).

Age	Male	Female	Both Sexes
Under 5 years	94100	91787	185887
5 to 9 years	84122	81955	166077
10 to 14 years	83274	81192	164466
15 to 19 years	91528	91405	182933
20 to 24 years	108407	114620	223027

pageSize:
set number of lines / page

Page buttons can
also be given labels

A live example is available at http://gvisapi-packt. appspot.com/ch5-examples/ch5-paging.html.

Dynamic or interactive

Animated transitions, the Chart Editor options, and dashboards can all be considered as either dynamic or interactive visualizations.

Animated transitions

The purpose of animated transitions with Chart Tools is to maintain a smooth transition between two different but very similar sets of data. For animations, two data sets must be supplied in order to make the before/after transition. The animation of the transition is triggered by an event, which is most often a user button-click. Animated transitions are a type of event control and are discussed further in *Chapter 7, Dashboards, Controls, and Events*.

The Animated Transitions documentation is available at https:// developers.google.com/chart/interactive/docs/animation.

Dashboards and controls

Although the topic of dashboards and controls has an entire chapter dedicated to its many applications, the concept of using a control mechanism to view data can be categorized as dynamic/interactive formatting. A dashboard is simply one or more real-time filter control(s) made available to the end user. In *Chapter 7, Dashboards, Controls, and Events*, the various aspects of end-user chart manipulation are covered in depth.

Chart Editor for users

It is possible to evoke the same Chart Editor used in Spreadsheets and Fusion Tables in an API-driven visualization. Unfortunately, the Chart Editor option only allows the Chart Wrapper (`wrapper.draw()`) method to be used to render the chart. If specific customization only available through `chart.draw()` is required, the Chart Wrapper limitations may become an issue. This topic is covered in additional detail in *Chapter 7, Dashboards, Controls, and Events*.

Summary

Formatting a chart can range from simple style choices of color to interactive displays manipulating the data view. In this chapter, relatively static formatting options were discussed. Interactive methods for formatting views of the data set were also introduced but not explored in detail. Additionally, the intertwined relationship of a dataset and formatting options became evident.

In the following chapters, both data resource management techniques and end-user interactive interfaces are explored in detail. The overall goal of the upcoming chapters is to present a comprehensive picture of the relationship between data, interactive interfaces, and style as a vehicle to convey meaning in a visualization.

6
Data Manipulation and Sources

Until now, data rendered in this book's examples have been defined within the code itself. Given this is a fairly limited method of storing data it naturally follows that a connection to external data sources must be developed. This chapter is dedicated to the topic of data accessibility for use in the Visualization API, including the following topics:

- Preparing/cleaning data
- Manipulating data with the Visualization API
- Configuring the following to be consumed as a data source:
  - Spreadsheets
  - Fusion Tables
- Manipulating data with their native APIs
- Apps Script equivalent functionality
- Creating your own data source

Data management is a topic that ranges well beyond the pages of this book, and the survey of methods presented in this chapter give only a handful of technical methods for working with data. This chapter is also not an exhaustive description of all Google data capabilities. For example, during the writing of this book, the Google Big Query (no SQL) and Prediction APIs are available as experimental options from the Apps Script development platform. It is very likely that as Google continues to further integrate API accessibility, additional data-focused APIs will emerge and become integrated as well. Also, beyond the tools provided by Google, traditional methods of database management are equally valid methods of data maintenance.

Preparing data

In general, it can be reasonably assumed that most collections of data are not as pristine as one would like them to be. Inconsistencies, poorly designed structures, and even mysterious extra whitespaces can be a nightmare for an average developer attempting to mine even the smallest amount of useful information. While not required, a best practice for data visualization is to first verify that the data to be visualized is formatted as expected.

Best practice

Before visualizing data, be sure it is arranged as expected and is free from inconsistencies.

The Google answer to the prevailing issue of dirty data is the free software tool, Google Refine. At the time of publication, Google Refine was in the process of transitioning from a Google Code hosted project to a GitHub hosted project called Open Refine. In either case, the capabilities and intentions of the tool remain the same. The application is a downloadable installation for Mac, Windows, and Linux operating systems. The stand-alone application is intentionally not a web service by design, as users with sensitive or private data can also use the tool without exposing their data on the Web. The intention of Google Refine is to provide the big picture of data, clean up messy raw data, and to discover and fix inconsistencies. It is particularly suited for public data, but can be used with any desired dataset.

The Google Refine documentation is available at `https://code.google.com/p/google-refine/`.
The Open Refine documentation is available at `http://openrefine.org/`.

Google Refine – importing data

Google Refine allows data of various formats and origins to be imported. The import wizard lists the formats Google Refine will accept. The application also allows for import from various locations, including Google Drive. The 2010 Chicago Census data that has been the subject of examples in the previous chapters can be imported into Refine from Google Drive by selecting **Google Data | Chicago_Census_2010_Ages** when signed into the Google Drive account used for previous examples.

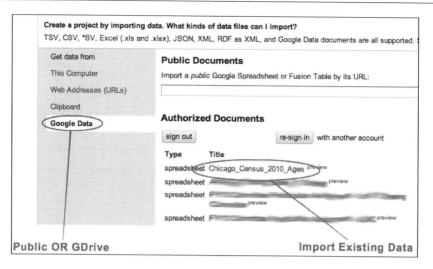

Google Refine – Facets

In Google Refine, a Facet is a feature or element of data. The primary capabilities of a Facet are two-fold. First, a Facet on a column of data allows the user to view the big picture of that column's data. Second, Facets are useful when a bulk change is to be performed on a subset of dataset values. To apply a Facet to a column, select the down arrow button to view general options for the column. Select **Facet** from the drop-down menu options, and then select whichever type of Facet is desired.

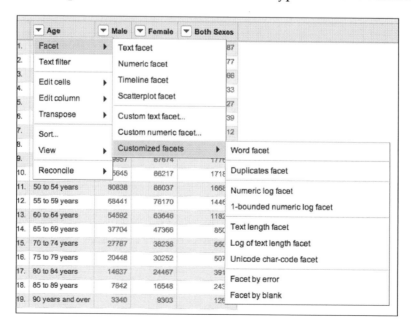

Google Refine contains a variety of Facets, but standard Facets can be described as similar to numeric or text-style filters. For users with unique requirements, custom Facets can be defined by using Google Refine Expression Language (GREL), Jython, and Clojure query languages. Selecting the **Customized facets** menu option opens up the dialog in which a custom query can be entered. References for the aforementioned query languages have been included at the end of this section, but their use is beyond the scope of this chapter.

Once a Facet has been selected or defined, it will appear as a window in the panel to the left of the primary application window. Facets are interactive in nature, and can be manipulated and deleted from the side panel location. The behavior of Facets is cumulative, which implies that the manipulation of one Facet applied to a section of data will also be reflected in other current Facets. This is the case in the following example where the U.S. 2010 Chicago Census data has been imported from Google Spreadsheets. Text and numeric Facets have been applied to the **Age** and **Male** columns, respectively. When the slider bars are adjusted to only select the two groups to the far right of the graph, the change is reflected in the **Age Facet** and two age categories are currently selected.

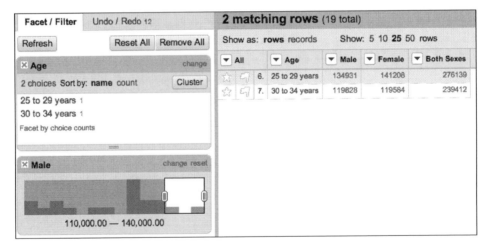

Google Refine – clean and supplement

Standard bulk operations to clean up messy data are fairly intuitive with Google Refine. For single cell edits, select the **Edit** button while hovering over a cell. The **Edit** button opens a dialog that allows editing of that cell. Options for bulk replace, changing the type of data in the cell, and editing the cell value itself are possible through the **Edit** option. Additional cell editing options are also available through the column's drop-down arrow menu under the **Edit cells** option.

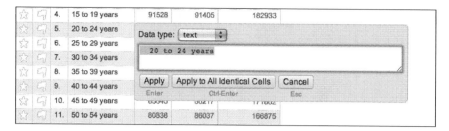

To make broader changes to a column's data, again select the down arrow in the column's label cell, this time choosing the **Edit column** option. In addition to the more standard column manipulations reminiscent of a Spreadsheet function, **Edit column** options can be used to collect additional information based on an existing column's values. A common use of this feature is the collection of latitude and longitude, also known as geocoding, information from an existing column of addresses. A third party service, such as Open Street Map's Nominatum, can be used by Google Refine to retrieve and store corresponding geocode information for each address in the data column. The Google Refine project home page hosts a how-to video on this and other Refine uses.

Finally, for anyone making sweeping changes to a dataset, the fear of making a change without the ability to retract is very real. It is also desirable to keep a record of operations performed on the data, just in case data transformations must be recreated. Google Refine provides an interactive history with redo/undo capability to address these concerns. To view the operation history, select the **Undo/Redo** tab, which can be found next to the **Facet/Filter** tab. The history actions are interactive, and simply selecting an operation in the history list will revert the dataset back to the specified state.

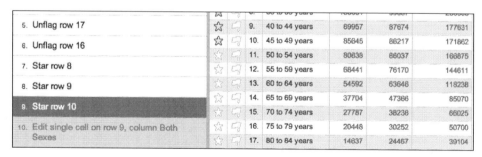

Google Refine – export options

Once a dataset has been modified as desired, Google Refine provides a variety of export options to deliver the newly cleaned data. Select the **Export** button to choose an export format.

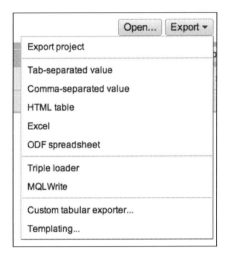

Alternatively, Google Refine is closely aligned with the Freebase open data repository, which is also an option for data export. To upload to Freebase, select the drop-down menu from the **Freebase** button directly below the **Export** button.

The Google Refine documentation is available at
`http://code.google.com/p/google-refine/`.

The Open Refine documentation is available at
`http://openrefine.org/`.

The Open Street Map Nominatim Service documentation is available
at `http://wiki.openstreetmap.org/wiki/Nominatim`.

The Jython Language documentation is available at
`http://www.jython.org/`.

The Clojure Language documentation is available at
`http://clojure.org/`.

The Freebase Open Data Repository documentation is available at
`http://www.freebase.org`.

Architecture and data modification

Before an external data source can be visualized in a chart, a translation from the data source format to a Visualization API-compatible format must be performed. The Visualization API does not directly handle the modification of the values stored in the dataset itself. The intention is not to be a data management tool, instead, the API environment provides a handful of programmatic methods to load selected data into the application. Once in a format it can understand, the Visualization API can manipulate any aspect of the data structure and content. In this way, the Visualization API is able to store initial data and any permutations for visualization purposes, but not become a tool for data source management.

Protocol

To translate between data sources and Visualization API applications, the data source must be "Visualization API-aware". There are several data source options already prepared to work with the Visualization API requests. These data sources may also have alternative methods of modification, such as manual entry or an API, but include the integrated ability to accept requests from the Visualization API.

Visualization API-ready data sources are as follows:

- Google Spreadsheets
- Google Fusion Tables

At first the idea of primarily using Spreadsheets and Fusion Tables as data sources appears very limiting. However, the additional feature of API integration makes these two applications fundamental for Google API-based applications. This is amplified by the fact that Google Apps are scalable, and performance enhancements are an inevitable aspect of the future. It is also very likely to be higher-powered data instances such as Google's SQL and Big Query which will eventually become Visualization API compatible by default. To strengthen this prediction, although efforts are still in experimental mode, API integration into the Apps Script environment is already available.

In the meantime, however, it is of course not realistic to assume that data can be confined to either Spreadsheets or Fusion Tables. Being able to directly query alternate sources from a Visualization API application is very desirable. To query datasets beyond Spreadsheets and Fusion Tables, the Visualization API provides a set of development libraries for the purpose of creating custom "Visualization-friendly" data sources. These libraries give developers the ability to integrate their own data source with the Visualization API protocol.

The process of retrieving information from a data source follows three general steps regardless of the data source type. First, the Visualization application must make a request for data from the data source. This operation occurs in the Visualization API command format. Next, the data source must interpret the application's request and assemble a response the Visualization code is able to understand, which is: `DataTable()`. The application receives the familiar `DataTable()` type as a response from the data source and can then use the response as usual.

The Visualization API can also interpret JSON objects, but this method requires slightly more handling by the developer than a returned `DataTable()`.

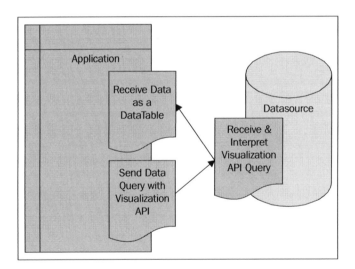

Visualization API data capabilities

As mentioned previously, retrieved data, in any format, is staged for visualization by the `DataTable()` class. In this book, `DataTable()` has so far been a necessary component of a visualization but has not been explicitly discussed. In simple examples for which data is a part of the application code, `DataTable()` is often observed in its `arrayDataTable()` helper function form, such as the case with simple area chart examples discussed in *Chapter 4, Basic Charts*.

```
var data = google.visualization.arrayToDataTable([
    ['Age', 'Male', 'Female', 'Both Sexes'],
    ['Under 5 years',    94100,       91787,        185887],
    ['5 to 9 years',     84122,       81955,        166077],
```

`DataTable()` also takes the form of `newDataTable()`, specifically in Google Apps Script applications, as illustrated in the following code snippet:

```
var data = Charts.newDataTable()
    .addColumn(Charts.ColumnType.STRING, "Age")
    .addColumn(Charts.ColumnType.NUMBER, "Male")
    .addColumn(Charts.ColumnType.NUMBER, "Female")
    .addColumn(Charts.ColumnType.NUMBER, "Both Sexes")
    .addRow(['Under 5 years', 94100,   91787,       185887])
    .addRow(['5 to 9 years',  84122,   81955,       166077])
```

`DataTable()` may seem like a simple component of a Visualization API script when presenting data from within the API script itself. Yet as data sources external to the script are introduced, the big picture role of `DataTable()` becomes increasingly important given its role as a data intermediary for external dataset query.

 Data Table reference is available at `https://developers.google.com/chart/interactive/docs/reference#DataTable`.

Group and join

Beyond simple database add/remove functionality, `DataTable()` also allows for
table grouping and joining capabilities. This functionality can be applied with a
`DataTable()` or between two separate `DataTable()` functions The **group** operation
sorts a `DataTable()` function's rows and then groups them together by column
value. In the following table, the 2010 Chicago Census data has several columns
that are in duplicate.

Dispersed Data

Age	Male	Female	Both Sexes
Under 5 years	94100	91787	185887
5 to 9 years	84122	81955	166077
5 to 9 years	0	0	0
10 to 14 years	83274	81192	164466
15 to 19 years	91528	91405	182933
20 to 24 years	108407	114620	223027
25 to 29 years	134931	0	0
25 to 29 years	0	141208	276139
30 to 34 years	119828	119584	239412
35 to 39 years	100651	99857	200508
40 to 44 years	89957	87674	177631
45 to 49 years	85645	86217	85931
45 to 49 years	85645	86217	85931
50 to 54 years	80838	86037	166875
55 to 59 years	68441	76170	144611

Consolidated Data

Age	Both Sexes
10 to 14 years	164466
15 to 19 years	182933
20 to 24 years	223027
25 to 29 years	276139
30 to 34 years	239412
35 to 39 years	200508
40 to 44 years	177631
45 to 49 years	171862
5 to 9 years	166077
50 to 54 years	166875
55 to 59 years	144611
Under 5 years	185887

The `DataTable().group` operation consolidates multiple rows in the table, and also sums the values of the rows that were combined. To do this, `group` needs to know on which column the consolidations should be defined. In this example, the first column (column [0]) is the **key**, or defining column for grouping. The `group` operation can also perform select other manipulations on a column when a consolidation of rows occurs. The example displays the sum of column three for the rows grouped together, and the existing value in the cell of column three if there is no grouping needed. The group option follows this syntax:

```
varmy_table = google.visualization.data.group(data_table, keys,
columns)
```

Here, `keys` is the column to group by, and `columns` provides additional parameters for which columns to display or perform a manipulation.

```
function drawGroup() {
   var data_table = google.visualization.arrayToDataTable([
         ['Age', 'Male', 'Female', 'Both Sexes'],
         ['Under 5 years',   94100,    91787,     185887],
         ['5 to 9 years',    84122,    81955,     166077],
         ['5 to 9 years',        0,        0,          0],
         ['10 to 14 years', 83274,    81192,     164466],
         ['15 to 19 years',   91528,    91405,     182933],
         ['20 to 24 years',  108407,  114620,     223027],
         ['25 to 29 years',  134931,        0,          0],
         ['25 to 29 years',        0,  141208,     276139],
         ['30 to 34 years',  119828,  119584,     239412],
         ['35 to 39 years',  100651,   99857,     200508],
         ['40 to 44 years',   89957,   87674,     177631],
         ['45 to 49 years',   85645,   86217,      85931],
         ['45 to 49 years',   85645,   86217,      85931],
         ['50 to 54 years',   80838,   86037,     166875],
         ['55 to 59 years',   68441,   76170,     144611]
      ]);

   // Group data_table by column 0, and show column 3 aggregated by sum.
   var grouped_dt = google.visualization.data.group(
         data_table, [0], [{'column': 3, 'aggregation':
         google.visualization.data.sum, 'type': 'number'}]);

   var table = new google.visualization.Table(document.
   getElementById('table'));
```

```
    table.draw(data_table, null);

    var grouped_table = new google.visualization.Table(document.
    getElementById('grouped_table'));
    grouped_table.draw(grouped_dt, null);
}
```

A **join** is another `DataTable()` operation that joins two separately defined `DataTables()` together. This type of manipulation is particularly useful when two datasets are available, each containing similar elements of the same item. For example, a table of census data with only male age groups could be combined with a similar table of the complementary female population by age group.

Male Population

Age	Male
Under 5 years	94100
5 to 9 years	84122
10 to 14 years	83274
15 to 19 years	91528
20 to 24 years	108407
25 to 29 years	134931
30 to 34 years	119828
35 to 39 years	100651
40 to 44 years	89957
45 to 49 years	85645
50 to 54 years	80838
55 to 59 years	68441

Female Population

Age	Female
Under 5 years	91787
5 to 9 years	81955
10 to 14 years	81192
15 to 19 years	91405
20 to 24 years	114620
25 to 29 years	141208
30 to 34 years	119584
35 to 39 years	99857
40 to 44 years	87674
45 to 49 years	86217
50 to 54 years	86037
55 to 59 years	76170

The preceding separate but complementary tables are joined to create a single combined table.

Both Sexes		
Age	Female	Male
10 to 14 years	81192	83274
15 to 19 years	91405	91528
20 to 24 years	114620	108407
25 to 29 years	141208	134931
30 to 34 years	119584	119828
35 to 39 years	99857	100651
40 to 44 years	87674	89957
45 to 49 years	86217	85645
5 to 9 years	81955	84122
50 to 54 years	86037	80838
55 to 59 years	76170	68441
Under 5 years	91787	94100

The syntax for a `DataTable().join` is as follows:

```
Var my_talble = google.visualization.data.join(table1, table2,
joinMethod, keys, table1Columns, table2Columns)
```

Here, `table1` and `table2` are the tables to be joined. The `joinMethod` function uses one of four possible parameters: `full/inner/left/right`.

- `full`: The output table includes all rows from both the tables, regardless of whether the keys match or not. Unmatched rows will have null cell entries; matched rows are joined.
- `inner`: This is a full join, but only includes rows where the keys match.
- `left`: The output table includes all rows from `data_table1`, whether or not there are any matching rows from `data_table2`.
- `right`: The output table includes all rows from `data_table2`, whether or not there are any matching rows from `data_table1`.

Keys is a set of definitions, which tells the join operation which columns to join as well as in what order the joins are to be performed. The syntax for keys is an array. table1Columns and table2Columns indicate which columns are to be displayed from each original table in the resulting joined table. These two configurations are also expressed as arrays. For example, the following code illustrates that the join operation is to be based on the comparison of the first column's values ([0,0] where one zero represents table1 table's first column and the other represents table2 table's first column). The second two bracketed 1's represent the original data table columns to be displayed along with the final joined table.

```
function drawJoin() {
var data_table1 = google.visualization.arrayToDataTable([
            ['Age', 'Male'],
            ['Under 5 years',    94100],
            ['5 to 9 years',     84122],
            ['10 to 14 years',   83274],
            ['15 to 19 years',   91528],
            ['20 to 24 years',   108407],
            ['25 to 29 years',   134931],
            ['30 to 34 years',   119828],
            ['35 to 39 years',   100651],
            ['40 to 44 years',   89957],
            ['45 to 49 years',   85645],
            ['50 to 54 years',   80838],
            ['55 to 59 years',   68441],
            ['60 to 64 years',   54592],
            ['65 to 69 years',   37704],
            ['70 to 74 years',   27787],
            ['75 to 79 years',   20448],
            ['80 to 84 years',   14637],
            ['85 to 89 years',   7842],
            ['90 years and over',3340]
        ]);

var data_table2 = google.visualization.arrayToDataTable([
            ['Age', 'Female'],
            ['Under 5 years',    91787],
            ['5 to 9 years',     81955],
            ['10 to 14 years',   81192],
            ['15 to 19 years',   91405],
            ['20 to 24 years',   114620],
            ['25 to 29 years',   141208],
            ['30 to 34 years',   119584],
            ['35 to 39 years',   99857],
```

```
            ['40 to 44 years',    87674],
            ['45 to 49 years',    86217],
            ['50 to 54 years',    86037],
            ['55 to 59 years',    76170],
            ['60 to 64 years',    63646],
            ['65 to 69 years',    47366],
            ['70 to 74 years',    38238],
            ['75 to 79 years',    30252],
            ['80 to 84 years',    24467],
            ['85 to 89 years',    16548],
            ['90 years and over',9303]
        ]);
```

```
// Create an full join of data_table1 and data_table2, using columns 0
as the key, include column 1 from both data tables
    var joined_dt = google.visualization.data.join(data_table2,
    data_table1, 'full', [[0,0]], [1], [1]);

    var table1 = new google.visualization.Table(document.
    getElementById('table1'));
        table1.draw(data_table1, null);

    var table2 = new google.visualization.Table(document.
    getElementById('table2'));
        table2.draw(data_table2, null);

    var joined_table = new google.visualization.Table(document.
    getElementById('joined_table'));
        joined_table.draw(joined_dt, null);
}
```

Information on Data Manipulation methods is available at
https://developers.google.com/chart/interactive/
docs/reference#google_visualization_data.

Live examples on Group is available at http://gvisapi-packt.
appspot.com/ch6-examples/ch6-group.html.

Live examples on Join is available at http://gvisapi-packt.
appspot.com/ch6-examples/ch6-join.html.

Spreadsheets

The primary method for manipulating data housed in the Spreadsheets application is through the application GUI itself. Since the Visualization API is not a data management editing interface, it is wrong to assume that an application will have adequate control over the data through `DataTable()` functionality. Rather, changes to the data stored in Spreadsheets must be accomplished through the GUI, Spreadsheets API, and forms.

Forms

Google Spreadsheets contains a form creation tool, which can be published to various destinations directly from the Spreadsheets application. Forms does not contain all of the advanced features of enterprise-class survey software, but is an easy-to-use data input method. To create a Spreadsheets Form, select **Tools | Create a form** from the menu bar.

In the form document that is created, use the **Add Item** button, found in-line with the form questions, to add additional questions to the form. Alternatively, select the **Insert** option from the menu bar to insert form questions.

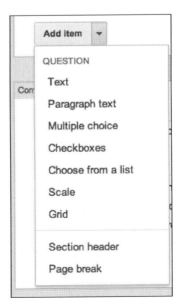

After adding the desired questions, publish the form to start collecting data. From the **File** menu, select an option for publication or sharing. The form can be published on the Google social networking site, Google+, emailed, embedded in a web page, or linked to form a web page.

To view the form live in a browser, locate the **View live form** button and click on it.

Forms can be edited after publication, and can be set to accept or reject new entries without damaging the existing data collected. Although remedial, forms are a powerful way to input data into a Visualization API-friendly data source.

API

The Spreadsheets API is accessible through the HTTP protocol, with client libraries available for Java and .NET. The HTTP methods consist primarily of **GET** and **POST** methods (RESTful), where data is structured with Google's custom XML namespace tags (`<gsx>`). For example, adding a row to the 2010 Census data, the `xmlns` entry would look something like the following code:

```
<entry xmlns="http://www.w3.org/2005/Atom"
    xmlns:gsx="http://schemas.google.com/spreadsheets/2006/extended">
  <gsx:age>30 to 32 years</gsx:age>
  <gsx:male>49</gsx:male>
  <gsx:female>51</gsx:female>
  <gsx:both_sexes>100</gsx:both_sexes>
</entry>
```

The preceding `row` entry would then be inserted via a **POST** message to the appropriate location in the Spreadsheet.

The manipulation of the Spreadsheets API is beyond the scope of this book, but more information can be found on Google's Spreadsheets API developer resource.

 Spreadsheets API reference is available at `https://developers.` `google.com/google-apps/spreadsheets/?hl=en`.

Fusion Tables – API

The Fusion Tables API is invoked through SQL-like queries. SQL is a special-purpose programming language designed for managing relational database systems. The Chart Tools Query Language discussed later in this chapter is intentionally very similar to SQL as SQL is a widely used standard language for data management.

 Fusion Tables API SQL Query reference is available at `https://developers.google.com/fusiontables/docs/v1/sql-reference`.

Data sources for Charts

The integrated nature of Spreadsheets and Fusion Tables as data sources make the coding of Charts with these external data sources for the Visualization API quite straightforward.

Spreadsheets

In Spreadsheets, two preparation steps must be addressed in order to use a Spreadsheet as a data source with the Visualization API. The first is to identify the URL location of the Spreadsheet file for the API code. The second step is to set appropriate access to the data held in the Spreadsheet file.

Preparation

The primary method of access for a Spreadsheet behaving as a data source is through a JavaScript-based URL query. The query itself is constructed with the Google Query Language (described in more detail later in this chapter). If the URL request does not include a query, all data source columns and rows are returned in their default order. To query a Spreadsheet also requires that the Spreadsheet file and the API application security settings are configured appropriately. Proper preparation of a Spreadsheet as a data source involves both setting the appropriate access as well as locating the file's query URL.

Permissions

In order for a Spreadsheet to return data to the Visualization API properly, access settings on the Spreadsheets file itself must allow view access to users. For a Spreadsheet that allows for edits, including form-based additions, permissions must be set to **Edit**. To set permissions on the Spreadsheet, select the **Share** button to open up the **Sharing settings** dialog. To be sure the data is accessible to the Visualization API, access levels for both the Visualization application and Spreadsheet must be the same. For instance, if a user has access to the Visualization application and does not have view access to the Spreadsheet, the user will not be able to run the visualization as the data is more restrictive to that user than the application. The opposite scenario is true as well, but less likely to cause confusion as a user unable to access the API application is a fairly self-described problem.

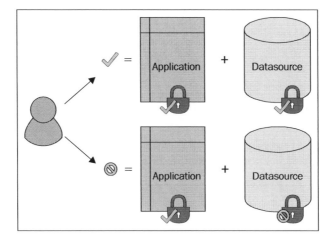

All Google applications handle access and permissions similarly. More information on this topic can be found on the Google Apps Support pages.

 Google Permissions overview is available at http://support.google.com/drive/bin/answer.py?hl=en&answer=2494886&rd=1.

Get the URL path

At present, acquiring a query-capable URL for a Spreadsheet is not as straightforward a task as one might think. There are several methods for which a URL is generated for sharing purposes, but *the* URL format needed for a data source query can only be found by creating a gadget in the Spreadsheet. A Google Gadget is simply dynamic, HTML or JavaScript-based web content that can be embedded in a web page. Google Gadgets also have their own API, and have capabilities beyond Spreadsheets applications.

 Information on Google Gadget API is available at
https://developers.google.com/gadgets/.

Initiate gadget creation by selecting the **Gadget...** option from the **Insert** item on the menu bar. When the **Gadget Settings** window appears, select **Apply & close** from the **Gadget Settings** dialog.

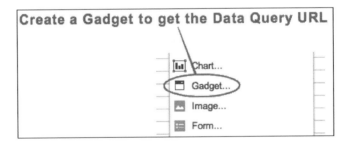

Choose any gadget from the selection window. The purpose of this procedure is simply to retrieve the correct URL for querying. In fact, deleting the gadget as soon as the URL is copied is completely acceptable. In other words, the specific gadget chosen is of no consequence.

Once the gadget has been created, select **Get query data source url...** from the newly created gadget's drop-down menu.

Next, determine and select the range of the Spreadsheet to query. Either the previously selected range when the gadget was created, or the entire sheet is acceptable, depending on the needs of the Visualization application being built. The URL listed under **Paste this as a gadget data source url** in the **Table query data source** window is the correct URL to use with the API code requiring query capabilities. Be sure to select the desired cell range, as the URL will change with various options.

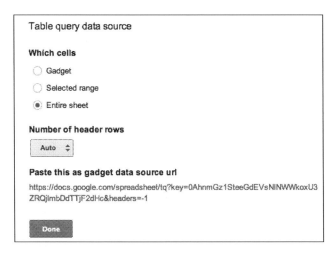

Important note

Google Gadgets are to be retired in 2013, but the query URL is still part of the gadget object at the time of publication. Look for the method of finding the query URL to change as Gadgets are retired.

Query

Use the URL retrieved from the Spreadsheet Gadget to build the query. The following query statement is set to query the entire Spreadsheet of the key indicated:

```
var query =
new google.visualization.Query(
'https://docs.google.com/spreadsheet/tq?key=0AhnmGz1SteeGdEVsNlNWWkoxU
3ZRQjlmbDdTTjF2dHc&headers=-1');
```

Once the query is built, it can then be sent. Since an external data source is by definition not always under explicit control of the developer, a valid response to a query is not necessarily guaranteed. In order to prevent hard-to-detect data-related issues, it is best to include a method of handling erroneous returns from the data source. The following `query.send` function also informs the application how to handle information returned from the data source, regardless of quality.

```
query.send(handleQueryResponse);
```

The `handleQueryResponse` function sent along with the query acts as a filter, catching and handling errors from the data source. If an error was detected, the `handleQueryResponse` function displays an alert message. If the response from the data source is valid, the function proceeds and draws the visualization.

```
function handleQueryResponse(response) {
    if (response.isError()) {
alert('Error in query: ' + response.getMessage() + ' ' + response.
getDetailedMessage());
      return;
    }
  var data = response.getDataTable();
  visualization = new google.visualization.Table
  (documnt.getElementById('visualization'));
  visualization.draw(data, null);
}
```

> **Best practice**
> Be prepared for potential errors by planning for how to handle them.

For reference, the previous example is given in its complete HTML form:

```
<html xmlns="http://www.w3.org/1999/xhtml">
  <head>
<meta http-equiv="content-type" content="text/html; charset=utf-8"/>
  <title>
  Google Visualization API Sample
  </title>
  <script type="text/javascript" src="http://www.google.com/jsapi">
  </script>
<script type="text/javascript">
    google.load('visualization', '1', {packages: ['table']});
  </script>
  <script type="text/javascript">
var visualization;
function drawVisualization() {
```

```
    // To see the data that this visualization uses, browse to
    // https://docs.google.com/spreadsheet/ccc?key=0AhnmGz1SteeGdEVsNlN
    WWkoxU3ZRQjlmbDdTTjF2dHc&usp=sharing

  var query = new google.visualization.Query(
          'https://docs.google.com/spreadsheet/tq?key=0AhnmGz1SteeGdEV
          sNlNWWkoxU3ZRQjlmbDdTTjF2dHc&headers=-1');

    // Send the query with a callback function.
    query.send(handleQueryResponse);
    }

function handleQueryResponse(response) {
    if (response.isError()) {
      alert('Error in query: ' + response.getMessage() + ' ' +
      response.getDetailedMessage());
      return;
    }

  var data = response.getDataTable();
      visualization = new google.visualization.Table(document.getEleme
      ntById('visualization'));
      visualization.draw(data, null);
}

    google.setOnLoadCallback(drawVisualization);

</script>
</head>
<body style="font-family: Arial;border: 0 none;">
    <div id="visualization" style="height: 400px; width: 400px;">
    </div>
  </body>
</html>
```

 View live examples for Spreadsheets at `http://gvisapi-packt.`
`appspot.com/ch6-examples/ch6-datasource.html`.

Apps Script method

Just as the Visualization API can be used from within an Apps Script, external data sources can also be requested from the script. In the Apps Script Spreadsheet example presented earlier in this book, the `DataTable()` creation was performed within the script. In the following example, the create data table element has been removed and a `.setDataSourceUrl` option has been added to `Charts. newAreaChart()`. The script otherwise remains the same.

```
functiondoGet() {

var chart = Charts.newAreaChart()
.setDataSourceUrl("https://docs.google.com/spreadsheet/tq?key=0AhnmGz1
SteeGdEVsN1NWWkoxU3ZRQjlmbDdTTjF2dHc&headers=-1")

.setDimensions(600, 400)
    .setXAxisTitle("Age Groups")
    .setYAxisTitle("Population")
    .setTitle("Chicago Population by Age and Gender - 2010 Census")
    .build();

varui = UiApp.createApplication();
ui.add(chart);
returnui;
}
```

 View live examples in Apps Script at `https://script. google.com/d/1Q2R72rGBnqPsgtOxUUME5zZy5Kul5 3r_lHIM2qaE45vZcTlFNXhTDqrr/edit.`

Fusion Tables

Fusion Tables are another viable data source ready for use by Visualization API. Fusion Tables offer benefit over Spreadsheets beyond just the Google Map functionality. Tables API also allows for easier data source modification than is available in Spreadsheets.

Preparation

Preparing a Fusion Table to be used as a source is similar in procedure to preparing a Spreadsheet as a data source. The Fusion Table must be shared to the intended audience, and a unique identifier must be gathered from the Fusion Tables application.

Permissions

Just as with Spreadsheets, Fusion Tables must allow a user a minimum of view permissions in order for an application using the Visualization API to work properly. From the **Sharing settings** window in Fusion Tables, give the appropriate users view access as a minimum.

Get the URL path

Referencing a Fusion Table is very similar in method to Spreadsheets. Luckily, the appropriate URL ID information is slightly easier to find in Fusion Tables than in Spreadsheets. With the **Sharing settings** window open, there is a field at the top of the page containing the **Link to share**. At the end portion of the link, following the characters **dcid=** is the Table's ID. The ID will look something like the following:

```
1Olo92KwNin8wB4PK_dBDS9eghe80_4kjMzOTSu0
```

This ID is the unique identifier for the table.

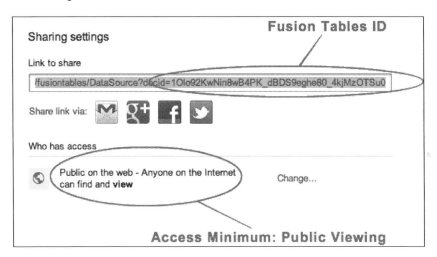

Query

Google Fusion Tables API includes SQL-like queries for the modification of Fusion Tables data from outside the GUI interface. Queries take the form of HTTP **POST** and **GET** requests and are constructed using the Fusion Tables API query capabilities. Data manipulation using Fusion Tables API is beyond the scope of this book, but a simple example is offered here as a basic illustration of functionality. Fusion Table query requests the use of the API SELECT option, formatted as:

```
SELECT Column_name FROM Table_ID
```

Here `Column_name` is the name of the Fusion Table column and `Table_ID` is the table's ID extracted from the **Sharing settings** window.

If the `SELECT` call is successful, the requested information is returned to the application in the JSON format. The Visualization API `drawChart()` is able to take the `SELECT` statement and the corresponding data source URL as options for the chart rendering. The male and female data from the Fusion Tables 2010 Chicago Census file have been visualized using the `drawChart()` technique.

```
function drawVisualization() {
       google.visualization.drawChart({
          containerId: 'visualization',
            dataSourceUrl: 'http://www.google.com/fusiontables/
            gvizdata?tq=',
          query: 'SELECT Age, Male, Female FROM 1Olo92KwNin8wB4PK_
          dBDS9eghe80_4kjMzOTSu0',
          chartType: 'AreaChart',
          options: {
            title: 'Chicago Population by Age and Sex - 2010 Census',
            vAxis: {
              title: 'Population'
            },
            hAxis: {
              title: 'Age Groups'
            }
          }
       });
}
```

The preceding code results in the following visualization:

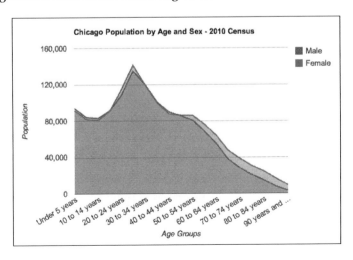

Live examples are available at `http://gvisapi-packt.` `appspot.com/ch6-examples/ch6-queryfusion.html`.

 Important note
Fusion Table query responses are limited to 500 rows. See Fusion Tables API documentation for other resource parameters.

API Explorer

With so many APIs available to developers using the Google platform, testing individual API functionality can be time consuming. The same issue arises for GUI applications used as a data source. Fortunately, Google provides API methods for its graphical applications as well. The ability to test API requests against Google's infrastructure is a desirable practice for all API programing efforts. To support this need, Google maintains the APIs Explorer service. This service is a console-based, web application that allows queries to be submitted to APIs directly, without an application to frame them.

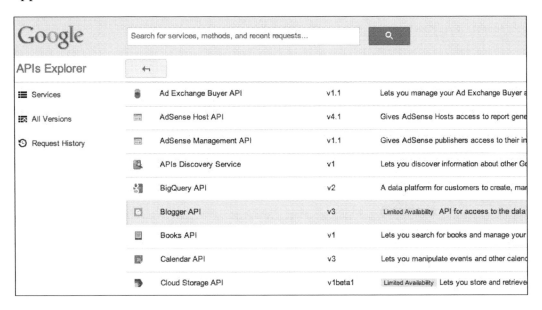

This is helpful functionality when attempting to verify whether a data source is properly configured. To check if the Fusion Tables 2010 U.S. Census data instance is configured properly, a query can be sent to list all columns, which informs which columns are actually exposed to the Visualization API application.

[**Best practice**
Use the Google API Explorer service to test if API queries work
as intended.]

To use the API Explorer for Fusion Tables, select **Fusion Tables API** from the list of
API services. API functions available for testing are listed on the Fusion Tables API
page. Troubleshooting a Chart with a Fusion Tables data source usually involves
first verifying all columns are available to the visualization code. If a column
is not available, or is not formatted as expected, a visualization issue related to
data problems may be difficult to troubleshoot from inside the Visualization API
environment. The API call that best performs a simple check on column information
is the `fusiontables.column.list` item.

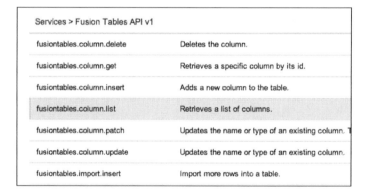

Selecting `fusiontables.column.list` opens up a form-based interface. The only
required information is the **Table ID** (collected from the **Share settings** window in
the Fusion Tables file). Click on the **Execute** button to run the query.

The API Explorer tool will then show the GET query sent to the Fusion Table in addition to the results it returned. For the `fusiontables.column.list` query, columns are returned in bracketed sections. Each section contains attributes of that column. The following queried attributes should look familiar, as it is the `fusiontables.column.list` result of a query to the 2010 Chicago Census data Fusion Table.

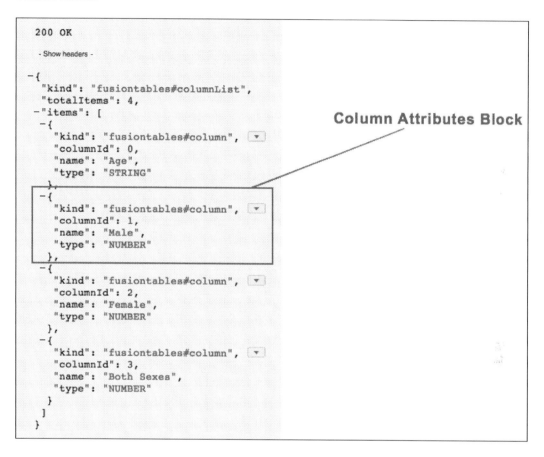

Best practice

The Column List Tool is helpful when troubleshooting Fusion Table to API code connectivity. If the Table is able to return coherent values through the tool, it can generally be assumed that access settings are appropriate and the code itself may be the source of connection issues.

Fusion Tables — row and query reference is available at `https://developers.google.com/fusiontables/docs/v1/sql-reference`.

Information on API Explorer — column list is available at `https://developers.google.com/fusiontables/docs/v1/reference/column/list#try-it`.

Chart Tools Query Language

The Visualization API query language (Chart Tools Query Language) is intended to provide developers with a method for mapping data from an external source to the various visualization data configuration requirements.

Just as with Spreadsheets and Fusion Tables data queries, the Chart Tools Query Language follows a SQL-like structure. An alternative to the URL query method is to set the query from within JavaScript, but the more common SQL method is represented by the following example. Set the query in JavaScript as follows:

```
var query = new google.visualization.Query(DATA_SOURCE_URL);
query.setQuery('select D where B > 50000);
query.send(handleQueryResponse);
```

The preceding query selects the item in column D only if the value in column B is greater than 50000. The same query can also be sent as part of the data source URL. There are four segments to a complete query formed as a URL. In the URL query:

- The http prefix:
    - `http://spreadsheets.google.com/a/google.com/tq?key=`
- Your:
    - `DATA_SOURCE_KEY`
- Segment to indicate a `select` statement is next:
    - `&tq=`
- The encoded `select` statement:
    - `select%20D%20where%20B%20%3E%2050000`

This results in the following query URL:

```
http://spreadsheets.google.com/a/google.com/tq?key=DATA_SOURCE_
KEY&tq=select%20D%20where%20B%20%3E%2050000
```

Use the web tool found in the Chart Tools Query Language documentation to encode or decode a query string.

Information on Query language reference and encode/decode tool is available at `https://developers.google.com/chart/ interactive/docs/querylanguage#Setting_the_Query_ in_the_Data_Source_URL`.

Build your own data source

Enabling a data source to work with the Visualization API requires some amount of programming experience. Java or Python development experience is ideal as the helper libraries available are written in these languages. However, it is also possible to create a data source from scratch. To create a reliable Visualization API-friendly data source, the prospective data source should meet several minimum requirements.

The data source should:

- Be available to clients
- Accept HTTP **GET** requests
- Handle unknown properties sent as part of requests (does not fail)
- Take proper security precautions regarding:
    ◦ Unknown clients
    ◦ Parsing expectations
- Make request and response strings UTF-8 encoded
- Support JSON first
- Document requirements for use

To make the addition of API compatibility easier, Google provides helper libraries in both Java and Python languages. The resulting task for the developer is then to be sure that the data source accurately relays its data to the helper library functions. The library functions will then relay the data, in an API-friendly format, to the application.

Spreadsheets as a data source reference is available at `https://developers.google.com/chart/interactive/docs/spreadsheets`.

Fusion Tables as a data source reference is available at `https://developers.google.com/chart/interactive/docs/fusiontables`.

Query Language reference is available at `https://developers.google.com/chart/interactive/docs/querylanguage`.

Chart Tools Data Source Protocol documentation is available at `https://developers.google.com/chart/interactive/docs/dev/implementing_data_source`.

Chart Tools data source library (Java) is available at `https://developers.google.com/chart/interactive/docs/dev/dsl_about`.

Chart Tools data source library (Python) is available at `https://developers.google.com/chart/interactive/docs/dev/gviz_api_lib`.

Summary

One of the biggest technology challenges of this decade is how to gain insight from seemingly unwieldy data collections. Often times the best method of enabling insight is the visualization of data. While the Visualization API does not modify data source values, it is capable of creating new elements from existing data. The visualization of both original and new data side-by-side, which is possible with the Visualization API, is a notable advantage. Another strength on which data analysts can capitalize is that the Visualization API includes both ready-to-use data source options as well as the necessary tools to retrofit your own data source.

Increasing the depth of data exploration through visualization also increases the need for interactive tools. The capability to filter data views on the fly also is a proven method of discovery that was not possible with static representations. The next chapter focuses on the interactive capabilities of the Visualization API through the use of the Dashboard option, viewing controls, and event triggers.

7
Dashboards, Controls, and Events

The previous chapter was dedicated to increasing the data capabilities of a visualization. This chapter discusses how to make customizable viewing options, allowing viewers to explore the visualization of data. Given that visualizations are such powerful tools, an increasing amount of scientific discovery is being attributed to data presented in exploratory visual environments. Even though the examples presented in this chapter are basic, it is feasible to extend Visualization API capabilities to more robust and complicated data models.

In this chapter we will cover:

- Architecture of a Visualization with a Dashboard
- Dashboard controls
- Event-based visualizations
- Transitioning between Visualizations with animation
- Chart editor for users

Architecture

The overall structure of a visualization with controls has slight but definitive differences from a chart without controls. For charts with controls, the HTML framework encasing the visualization is slightly modified, as is the method of drawing the visualization with the API. The modified HTML framework is a good starting point to describe the architecture of a visualization with control components.

HTML framework

The HTML structure of a visualization with controls is similar to the standard HTML visualization framework, with a few distinct alterations. Dashboards require a few small changes to the HTML `<body>` section of the page. As with visualizations themselves, a `<div id>` must be designated for not only the chart, but also each of the Dashboard and control elements. An advantage to separately assigned `<div id>` tags is the Dashboard, control, and chart components that can be placed as desired in a page stylized with conventional HTML methods.

To start with, in the `<head>` section, a small change must be made to the line indicating which chart library is to be loaded. In any standard visualization using the `chart.draw()` method, a Google library must always be identified in the code in order for the appropriate visualization components to be loaded. The key difference for a chart with controls is that the visualization uses the `ChartWrapper` class, rather than the `chart.draw()` method, to package the controls and chart together. This means the library declaration that is used not only loads the mechanisms to create and link control elements, but also loads the mechanisms to draw the charts themselves. The `controls` library packaged is loaded using the `google.load` command.

```
google.load('visualization', '1.0',{'packages':['controls']});
```

API framework

Along with an alternative library load requirement, there are also several changes in the API execution of the visualization with chart controls. When creating one or more controls for a chart, the controllers and data must be logically linked together in order to alter the view of the chart on the fly. This bundling function is accomplished through the use of the Dashboard component. **Dashboards** are the encapsulation that holds the controls, data, and chart together as a single visualization. The encapsulation of all of these elements requires a slightly different method of chart creation as well. The `ChartWrapper` class, introduced briefly in *Chapter 2, Anatomy of a Visualization,* is the prescribed method when drawing charts with controls. The `ChartWrapper` class is analogous to `chart.draw()`, but is intended as a helper or bundling method to simplify drawing chart components. It packages together the handling of the data source, chart libraries, and drawing for the visualization. This simplification does potentially limit chart drawing customization options when compared to `chart.draw()`, but is the Google recommended method for including Dashboards and controls in a visualization, given the increased simplicity of deployment.

Additionally, to perform the bundling task for the Dashboard, the `bind` function is used to designate the link from charts and controls to the Dashboard. Once the controls and chart visualization variables have been created, `bind` is used to bundle each of the objects together prior to the Dashboard's `draw` process.

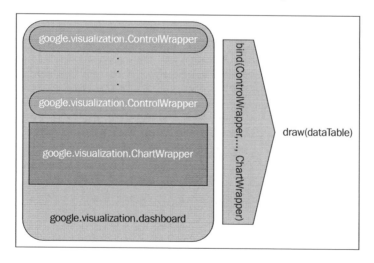

ControlWrapper

In the preceding figure, the ChartWrapper and ControlWrapper classes both have their own declaration in the Visualization API environment. The result of ChartWrapper is, of course, a chart. In a similar manner a ControlWrapper class equates to a handful of possible user controls: StringFilter, NumberRangeFilter, ChartRangeFilter, and CategoryFilter.

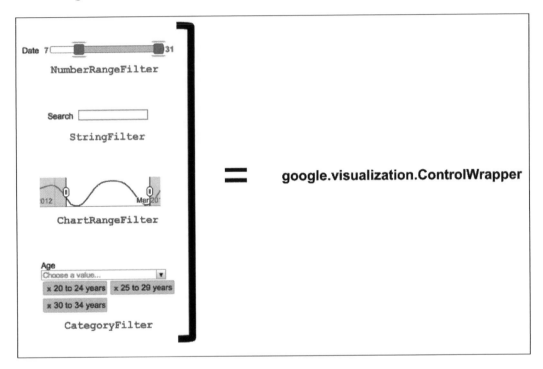

Details regarding functionality for each of these control filter options are discussed in the *Dashboard – controls* section of this chapter.

ChartWrapper

ChartWrapper handles tasks associated with the chart creation itself. These tasks are as follows:

- Load
- Draw
- Data source
- Events

In particular, the `ChartWrapper` class has its own methods for setting chart attributes and values. It also does not require a callback function to be declared, as would be the case with `chart.draw`. Instead `ChartWrapper` handles the callback as part of the data source query. For larger visualizations with a variety of charts, the `ChartWrapper` helper class dynamically loads chart libraries, rather than requiring each individual library to be declared in the code.

Load

As mentioned in the *HTML framework* section of this chapter, the `google.load` command with the `'controls'` package is required in the HTML portion of the visualization code. The following two lines load the JavaScript API into the visualization. The next line is the `google.load` declaration for the Visualization `controls` library. Both the JavaScript API library and subsequent controls library must be present in order for visualizations with controls to function.

```
<script type="text/javascript" src="http://www.google.com/jsapi"></
script>

<script type="text/javascript">
google.load('visualization', '1.1', {packages: ['controls']});
```

Important

In general, an alternative to loading the appropriate libraries manually for `ChartWrapper` is to load them dynamically. The dynamic method does *NOT* replace the loading of the control library for charts with controls and dashboards. This method is intended for `ChartWrapper` charts that do not include dashboards or controls at this time.

For reference only, to dynamically load chart libraries for a visualization with no controls or dashboard, use the following code:

```
<script type="text/javascript"src='https://www.google.com/jsapi?autolo
ad={"modules":[{"name":"visualization","version":"1"}]}'>
</script>
```

Use the previous code in replacement of the `jsapi` and `google.load` lines of a `ChartWrapper` chart without controls. Once again note this information has been provided for reference only in this section, and will not work properly with charts using dashboards and controls.

Data source

As mentioned in *Chapter 6, Data Manipulation and Sources,* Google Visualizations can accept a variety of data sources. The tradeoff to this flexibility is a translation step that is required when loading data from a data source to a chart. Sometimes the translation is easy yet some must be built, as is the case with using the API `DataTable` object. Other cases require some additional programming to properly align the data source and the visualization's formatting expectations. A benefit of the `ChartWrapper` helper function is the built-in streamlined access to several data sources. In particular, `ChartWrapper` has the ability to handle JSON strings directly. There is also a small assortment of data-related commands in `ChartWrapper` that can simplify initiating and then querying a data source. The most frequently used commands are as follows:

* `setQuery(query_string)`
* `setDataSourceUrl(url)`
* `getDataTable()`
* `setDataTable(table)`

Draw

The declaration and drawing method for `ChartWrapper` is very similar to the `chart.draw()` function. In fact, on the surface, the primary difference between the two is simply the organization of the declaration. For example, both `chart.draw()` and `ChartWrapper` are set to a variable such that additional methods may be invoked using the variable. In more detail, the difference becomes apparent in the execution of the two methods. The `chart.draw()` method returns a chart and uses the variable as a reference, where `ChartWrapper` only uses the variable as a reference to the Chart Wrapper function.

Using `chart.draw()`:

```
varmychart = new google.visualization.LineChart(document.getElementByI
D('visualization').
        draw(data, {curveType: "function",
                    width: 500, height: 400}
```

or, using `ChartWrapper`:

```
var wrapper = new google.visualization.ChartWrapper({
  chartType: 'LineChart',
  options: {'curveType': 'function',
  'width': 500, 'height': 400},
  containerId: 'visualization'
});
wrapper.draw();
```

Both methods produce identical charts. To break down the `ChartWrapper` declaration even further, the key components of the `ChartWrapper` declaration are listed as follows:

The setup process for the `draw` function is:

- `setChartType(type)`
    - set a *chart type* (example: line, bar, or area)

- `setOption(key, value)`
    - set *chart options* that are specific to the type of chart chosen

- `getContainerId(id)`
    - tell `ChartWrapper` where to draw the chart through retrieving the `ContainerId`

- `draw(opt_container_ref)`
    - draw the chart using the `draw()` attribute

Events

As an added feature of the `ChartWrapper` class method, developers are given in-built control to a standard set of messages outputted from `ChartWrapper`. The message availability is provided in order to enable additional functionality to a visualization application. When working with events, it is important to keep in mind that, in order for any event to occur, the `draw()` function must have occurred first, as it generates the event messages.

The three types of messages generated by `ChartWrapper` are:

- Error
- Ready
- Select

Error

An **error event** is a message that results from an issue occurring during the rendering of the chart visualization itself.

Ready

The **ready event** primarily functions as a method for acknowledging user input from a visualized chart. When an input function occurs, such as a mouse click, the application reacts to the click and performs the designated section of code. This type of event must be declared prior to calling the `ChartWrapperdraw()` function.

Select

Using the **select event** is not completely intuitive as its purpose is to return the location of the user's selection *in the visualization chart itself.* That is, HTML selection events outside the visualization are not detected and returned as a select event. Instead, the purpose of a select event is to return a notification to the application when a user selects a bar or legend of the visualization.

Troubleshooting

The ready event must be declared prior to the execution of draw().

All events (error/ready/select) use the same method for declaration. The following is the function that sets up a specific event. The chart being drawn, type of event (error/ready/select), and subsequent action to take, are defined as options in the declaration. The following code creates an event that *listens* for event_type to occur. When the event occurs, the code then instructs to execute the run_on_event function.

```
Google.visualization.events.addListener(wrapper, 'event_type', run_on_
event);
```

The anatomy of the function run when the event is triggered, run_on_event, is strikingly similar to the general anatomy of a visualization function, or any other JavaScript function. Just as with a visualization, the event handling code is encapsulated entirely in a function of its own. Event functions are not included in the visualization function, but are standalone entities between the <script> tags in the application code. The run_on_event function here sends an alert to the user that the chart failed to draw.

```
// Run this when the 'error' event occurs!

function run_on_event() {
alert("Chart failed to draw!");  }
}
```

It is helpful to think of functions that call other functions as a call and response process. The purpose of the event listener inside the visualization function is to literally *listen* for the specified event to occur. When it does occur, the listener *calls* to the responder function outside of the visualization code section. The responder function then executes its code, which concludes the call and then the response. Events are a useful tool in particular when designing visualizations to respond to user selections.

Dashboards

Dashboards are the backdrops on which all controls and charts are bundled together. Since they act as the unifying component of the visualization and controls, dashboards can also be intentionally linked to create dependencies between controls. Controls may also be used to set a visualization to a predefined state, or act as a trigger point for `ChartWrapper` events.

In general, a visualization with dashboard, controls, and events will always follow a pattern similar to the following outline:

```
<html>
<head>
<script>
function visualization{

// Listen for an error event to happen
google.visualization.events.addListener(chart/dashboard, 'error/ready/
select',run_on_error);

// Load the Wrapper libraries
google.load


// Data creation, linking methods don't change
var data = google.visualization.DataTable

// Create some controls
var ctrl = new google.visualization.ControlWrapper


// Create a chart
var chart = new google.visualization.ChartWrapper

// Bundle controls and charts together on a dashboard. Draw the
visualization.
google.visualization.Dashboard
bind( )

draw(data)
```

```
}

// Run this function when addListener "hears" the event
function run_on_error{

}
</script>
</head>
.
.
.
</html>
```

Now that it's possible to create "triggers" to listen for events in the dashboard, it is useful to harness the triggering ability through the user interface. With the Visualization API, the API controls as well as standard JavaScript interactivity, such as `onload` and `onclick`, are accepted methods to initiate chart events from the user interface.

Controls

The purpose of `ControlWrapper` controls is to allow the viewer to manipulate the chart data into their own desired visualization using on-screen graphical methods. Controls do not alter the dataset itself, but instead provide a filtered view only. This method is desirable to both developer and user as it presents anyone viewing the chart to customize the visualization to their needs sans concern of damaging the visualization or data by doing so.

There are several kinds of filters available:

- `StringFilter`
- `NumberRangeFilter`
- `CategoryFilter`
- `ChartRangeFilter`

StringFilter

`StringFilter` control is essentially a search filter for the data table. The user enters strings of characters as search queries into a field, and the visualization dynamically displays the results of the search. The `StringFilter` control is defined using the `ControlWrapper` method:

```
varMyFilter = google.visualization.ControlWrapper({
    'controlType': 'StringFilter',
```

```
    'containerId': 'control1',
    'options': {
      'filterColumnLabel': 'your_column_name'
    }
  });
```

The following chart example presents the same 2010 Chicago Census data that has been a continuing resource throughout this book. However, in this case, only the data for the male population is used. In the example, users may enter a sequence of numbers in the search field, and the chart view is reduced to only those entries where the sequence of numbers exists in the **Male** column.

Age	Male
Under 5 years	94100
5 to 9 years	84122
10 to 14 years	83274
15 to 19 years	91528
20 to 24 years	108407
25 to 29 years	134931
30 to 34 years	119828
35 to 39 years	100651
40 to 44 years	89957

The preceding data for age groups of males is loaded into the visualization with the `arrayToDataTable` function. Of course, an alternative method would be to use a data source method as described in *Chapter 6, Data Manipulation and Sources*, such as a Spreadsheet URL or JSON feed. If a data source method is chosen, remember that the `ChartWrapper` function used for charts with controls provides the data source linkage methods within `ChartWrapper`. The following data array is created in the example chart's script.

```
['Age', 'Male'],
['Under 5 years',   94100],
['5 to 9 years',    84122],
['10 to 14 years',  83274],
['15 to 19 years',  91528],
['20 to 24 years',  108407],
['25 to 29 years',  134931],
['30 to 34 years',  119828],
['35 to 39 years',  100651],
['40 to 44 years',  89957],
['45 to 49 years',  85645],
['50 to 54 years',  80838],
['55 to 59 years',  68441]
```

As mentioned earlier in the chapter, when building dashboards, the control elements and chart must be defined first. To define the control for the `StringFilter`, use the `ControlWrapper` class to create the object with the `StringFilter` control being the `controlType`. Also, define which `<div id>` element you wish to use as a container. The `containerID` option sets the `<div id>`, anchoring the control to the HTML page. Control has a variety of variables that can be set at the time of declaration, most of them being optional. However, for the `StringFilter` control in this instance, a column index or label is required in order for the control to know on which column to apply the search. This is accomplished by the addition of the `filterColumnLabel` option which provides the the filter's definition. In the example, the filter is set to search on the **Male** column.

```
// Define a StringFilter control for the 'Male Population' column
var stringFilter = new google.visualization.ControlWrapper({
    'controlType': 'StringFilter',
    'containerId': 'control1',
    'options': {
      'filterColumnLabel': 'Male'
    }
});
```

Now that the search filter has been defined, the chart itself must be configured. In this example, a table visualization is the end result. To build the table and make it compatible with the controls just defined, use the `ChartWrapper` class. When defining `ChartWrapper`, configure `chartType`, the `<div id>` container HTML element, in addition to other formatting.

```
// Define a table visualization
var table = new google.visualization.ChartWrapper({
   'chartType': 'Table',
   'containerId': 'mydivid',
   'options': {'height': '13em', 'width': '20em'}
});
```

To complete the dashboard, the `ControlWrapper` and `ChartWrapper` components must be assigned to the dashboard component. This is accomplished through the `bind` function. The semantics for `bind` are to first state the control to be bound in parentheses; with the data object it is to be bound to as the second input variable. The `bind` function may also be used in series to create dependent controls that manipulate the same visualization. Dependent controls are a topic covered later in this chapter.

```
// Create the dashboard.
var dashboard = new google.visualization.Dashboard(document.
getElementById('dashboard')).
   // Configure the string filter to affect the table contents
   bind(stringFilter, table).
   // Draw the dashboard
   draw(data);
```

For reference, the following code example for a `StringFilter` control is presented in its entirety, including the HTML framework.

```
<!DOCTYPE html PUBLIC "-//W3C//DTD XHTML 1.0 Strict//EN" "http://www.
w3.org/TR/xhtml1/DTD/xhtml1-strict.dtd">
<html xmlns="http://www.w3.org/1999/xhtml">
 <head>
  <meta http-equiv="content-type" content="text/html; charset=utf-8"/>
   <title>
   Google Visualization API Sample
   </title>
   <script type="text/javascript" src="http://www.google.com/jsapi">
   </script>
   <script type="text/javascript">
     google.load('visualization', '1.1', {packages: ['controls']});
   </script>
   <script type="text/javascript">
   function drawVisualization() {
       // Prepare the data.
     var data = google.visualization.arrayToDataTable([
             ['Age', 'Male'],
             ['Under 5 years',    94100],
             ['5 to 9 years',     84122],
             ['10 to 14 years',   83274],
             ['15 to 19 years',   91528],
             ['20 to 24 years',  108407],
             ['25 to 29 years',  134931],
             ['30 to 34 years',  119828],
```

```
                  ['35 to 39 years',    100651],
                  ['40 to 44 years',     89957],
                  ['45 to 49 years',     85645],
                  ['50 to 54 years',     80838],
                  ['55 to 59 years',     68441]
        ]);

      // Define a StringFilter control for the 'Male Population'
      column
      var stringFilter = new google.visualization.ControlWrapper({
         'controlType': 'StringFilter',
         'containerId': 'control1',
         'options': {
           'filterColumnLabel': 'Male'
         }
      });

      // Define a table visualization
      var table = new google.visualization.ChartWrapper({
         'chartType': 'Table',
         'containerId': 'chart1',
         'options': {'height': '13em', 'width': '20em'}
      });

      // Create the dashboard.
      var dashboard = new google.visualization.Dashboard(document.
      getElementById('dashboard')).
         // Configure the string filter to affect the table contents
         bind(stringFilter, table).
         // Draw the dashboard
         draw(data);
     }

    google.setOnLoadCallback(drawVisualization);
  </script>
</head>
<body style="font-family: Arial;border: 0 none;">
  <div id="dashboard">
    <table>
      <tr style='vertical-align: top'>
        <td style='width: 300px; font-size: 0.9em;'>
```

```
            <div id="control1"></div>
            <div id="control2"></div>
            <div id="control3"></div>
          </td>
          <td style='width: 600px'>
            <div style="float: left;" id="chart1"></div>
          </td>
        </tr>
      </table>
    </div>
  </body>
</html>
```

Predictability of a control

Before publishing a visualization with controls, it is important to understand how the control actually affects the data view. This may be common sense, but can be an easily overlooked step. Often it may be assumed a filter will behave a certain way, when in reality the actual behavior is quite different. In the following example, the number "1" is entered into the search field. The resulting filter of data returns all entries in the **Male** column that begins with the integer 1. An incorrect interpretation of this filter functionality may have been to search the column for the number 1 as it appears anywhere, even numerous times, in the entry.

Male	1		Age	Male
			20 to 24 years	108407
			25 to 29 years	134931
			30 to 34 years	119828
			35 to 39 years	100651

Similarly, searching for 10 returns only the population numbers that start with 10. Entries that contain other sequences or alternative string locations, such as 180 or 2010 are not among the results.

Male	10		Age	Male
			20 to 24 years	108407
			35 to 39 years	100651

At this point, it can be assumed searching for the string `108` will only return the exact sequence of the integer one, followed by the integer zero, followed by the integer eight, which is in fact, the result.

At the time of this publication, the Visualization API does not support using the generally accepted notation of language processing searches, such as wildcards and ranges that do not improve results. At this time, it can then be deduced that the `StringFilter` is literally just that, a simple string filter. In this case, the filter may sometimes behave as a search-style control, but is actually not designed for typical search functionality.

 Live examples can be found at `http://gvisapi-packt.appspot.com/ch7-examples/ch7-stringfilter.html`.

Overall, adding controls to a chart is fairly simple. Issues primarily arise when expectations of a certain functionality do not coincide with actual functionality.

 Know how `ControlWrapper` controls interact with specific charts and data. Test control functionality to be sure that the visualization result is as expected and intended.

NumberRangeFilter

A `NumberRangeFilter` control is a bar-shaped slider with handles at each end of the bar. The individual viewing the chart is able to manipulate the handles in order to dynamically view a specific range of data on the visualization.

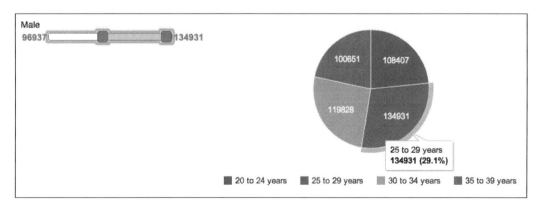

A `NumberRangeFilter` is built in the same manner as a `StringFilter`. First, the control object for the filter is defined. Notice much of the code is exactly the same, with the exception of the `controlType` setting. To create a `NumberRangeFilter`, create the same object as with `StringFilter` but substitute `NumberRangeFilter` as the `controlType`.

```
// Define a slider control for the 'Male Population' column
  var slider = new google.visualization.ControlWrapper({
    'controlType': 'NumberRangeFilter',
    'containerId': 'control1',
    'options': {
      'filterColumnLabel': 'Male',
      'ui': {'labelStacking': 'vertical'}
    }
  });
```

Once again, as with `StringFilter`, create the chart component for the `NumberRangeFilter`.

```
var piechart = new google.visualization.ChartWrapper({
'chartType': 'PieChart',
 'containerId': 'chart1',
 'options': {
   'width': 700,
   'height': 300,
   'legend': 'bottom',
'chartArea': {'left': 15, 'top': 15, 'right': 0, 'bottom': 0},
     'pieSliceText': 'value'
   }
});
```

Finally, finalize the drawing of the chart by attaching the control to the visualization dashboard component with `bind`.

```
// Create the dashboard.
new google.visualization.Dashboard(document.
getElementById('dashboard')).
   // Configure the slider to affect the piechart
   bind(slider, piechart).
   // Draw the dashboard
   draw(data);
```

 Live examples are available at `http://gvisapi-packt.appspot.com/ch7-examples/ch7-numrange.html`.

CategoryFilter

A `CategoryFilter` control is a drop-down menu where selecting an item from the drop-down filters the view of the visualization based on that selected item. `CategoryFilter` has several customization options, such as allowing multiple selections at a time, or user-typed selections. The following example shows a category filter that sets the chart view by selected age group.

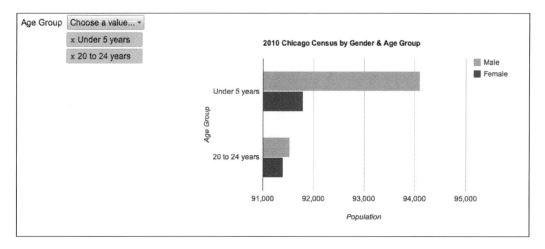

To illustrate the power of visualization when using a category filter, note in the preceding figure, the **Under 5 years** and **20 to 24 years** categories make chart data appear relatively close in value. However, when a third, **25 to 29 years** category is added, values of data are not as close as first suggested.

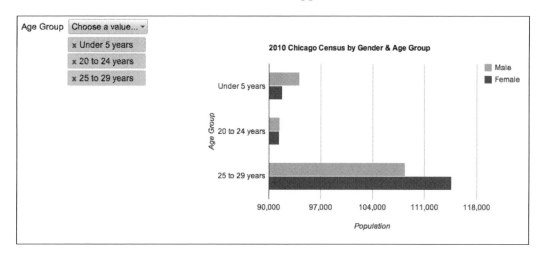

Using `CategoryFilter` controls allow users to target specific regions of data without losing the perspective of the entire dataset. The `CategoryFilter` control is created in a similar manner to other controls. As with any other visualization, create or import data first.

```
function drawVisualization() {
  // Prepare the data.
  var data = google.visualization.arrayToDataTable([
    ['Age Group', 'Male', 'Female'],
    ['Under 5 years', 94100, 91787],
    ['10 to 14 years', 84122, 81955],
    ['15 to 19 years', 83274, 81192],
    ['20 to 24 years', 91528, 91405],
    ['25 to 29 years', 108407, 114620],
    ['30 to 24 years', 134931, 141208]
  ]);
```

Then, a variable is defined to provide the age selector control. The control creation also defines an initial state for the chart.

```
  // Define a category picker for the Age Group column.
  var agePicker = new google.visualization.ControlWrapper({
    'controlType': 'CategoryFilter',
    'containerId': 'control1',
    'options': {
      'filterColumnLabel': 'Age Group',
      'ui': {
        'allowTyping': false,
        'allowMultiple': true,
        'selectedValuesLayout': 'belowStacked'
      }
    },
    // Define an initial state, i.e. a set of age groups to be
    initially selected.
    'state': {'selectedValues': ['Under 5 years', '20 to 24 years']}
  });
```

Following the control creation, the bar chart visualization must be defined. The label options for the chart are included as part of the `options` definitions.

```
  // Define a bar chart with ChartWrapper.
  var barChart = new google.visualization.ChartWrapper({
    'chartType': 'BarChart',
    'containerId': 'chart1',
    'options': {
      'colors': ['orange', 'purple'],
```

```
        'title': ['2010 Chicago Census by Gender & Age Group'],
        'hAxis':{'title': "Population"},
        'vAxis':{'title': "Age Group"},
        'width': 550,
        'height': 350
    }
});
```

Finally, the dashboard is created and the `bind` function links the selection control and chart together.

```
    // Create the dashboard.
    var dashboard = new google.visualization.Dashboard(document.
    getElementById('dashboard')).
        // Configure the age picker to affect the chart
        bind(agePicker, barChart).
        // Draw the dashboard
        draw(data);
}
```

 Live examples are available at `http://gvisapi-packt.appspot.com/ch7-examples/ch7-catfilter.html`.

ChartRangeFilter

Similar to the `NumberRangeFilter` control that filters a data view based on a column's range of values, the `ChartRangeFilter` control filters a view based on a time period.

`ChartRangeFilter` involves time-based data, which requires extra discussion. Given this need, it is better categorized as part of the *Time-based charts* section in *Chapter 8, Advanced Charts*. The following graphic is a `ChartRangeFilter` control filtering the main chart view data that is linked to a time period in roughly February 2012.

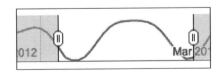

Controls with dependencies

A series of controls may be linked together, such that the subsequent control relies on the previous control's value. Outside of the Visualization API, this is often referred to as a cascading list of values. This technique is particularly useful with charts that require a selection of data to be systematically pared down from larger categories. A control that filters by country may then become a dependency of another control that filters by state, city, or county. The state filter will automatically receive the filtered results of the country control as its selection options. In this way, it is possible to view data at various levels of granularity by using multiple controls in conjunction.

To illustrate, this is a simple bar graph that has been created from the age group population data of Chicago from 2000, 2005, and 2010. One of the controls on the far-left side has a dependency on the other. When the **Year** is selected, the graph is populated with that particular year's population for the selected year. To further filter the display, one or more **Age Groups** may be selected for the given year.

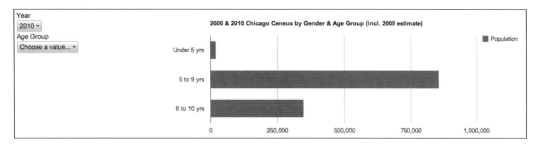

To change the selected data to another year, simply select the **Year** drop-down and pick a different option. The data displayed will automatically adjust to the **Age Group** filters already selected. The following dependency example is in its entirety. On initial load, the **Year** option has been preset to 2010. Setting of the initial state takes place as part of the control declaration itself.

```
function drawVisualization() {
  // Prepare the data
  var data = google.visualization.arrayToDataTable([
    ['Year', 'Age Group', 'Population'],
    ['2000', 'Under 5 yrs', 776733],
    ['2005', 'Under 5 yrs', 8175173],
    ['2010', 'Under 5 yrs', 21372],
    ['2000', '5 to 9 yrs', 3694820],
    ['2005', '5 to 9 yrs', 70708],
    ['2010', '5 to 9 yrs', 857592],
    ['2000', '6 to 10 yrs', 2193031],
    ['2005', '6 to 10 yrs', 852395],
```

```
      ['2010', '6 to 10 yrs', 348556]
  ]);
  var yearPicker = new google.visualization.ControlWrapper({
    'controlType': 'CategoryFilter',
    'containerId': 'control2',
    'options': {
      'filterColumnLabel': 'Year',
      'ui': {
        'labelStacking': 'vertical',
        'allowTyping': false,
        'allowMultiple': false
      }
    },
    'state': {'selectedValues': ['2010']}
  });
  var agePicker = new google.visualization.ControlWrapper({
    'controlType': 'CategoryFilter',
    'containerId': 'control3',
    'options': {
      'filterColumnLabel': 'Age Group',
      'ui': {
        'labelStacking': 'vertical',
        'allowTyping': false,
        'allowMultiple': true
      }
    }
  });

  // Define a bar chart to show 'Population' data
  var barChart = new google.visualization.ChartWrapper({
    'chartType': 'BarChart',
    'containerId': 'chart1',
    'options': {
      'title': ['2000 & 2010 Chicago Census by Gender & Age Group
      (incl. 2005 estimate)'],
      'width': 800,
      'height': 300,
      'chartArea': {top: 50, right: 50, bottom: 50}
    },
    // Configure the barchart to use columns 1 (age group) and 2
    (population)
    'view': {'columns': [1, 2]}
```

```
    });

    // Create the dashboard.
    new google.visualization.Dashboard(document.
    getElementById('dashboard')).
      // Configure the controls so that:
      // - the 'Year' selection drives the 'Age Group' one,
      // - and the 'Age Group' output drives the chart

      bind(yearPicker, agePicker).
      bind(agePicker, barChart).
      // Draw the dashboard
      draw(data);
}
```

 Live examples can be found at http://gvisapi-packt.
appspot.com/ch7-examples/ch7-dependentctrl.html.

Working with dependent controls may take some trial and error to make them function as desired.

Troubleshooting

When using the ChartArea option in defining a chart, be careful to not make area values too small so that title and axis labels are accidentally cropped out of the viewable area. If titles or axis labels do not appear as expected, try increasing the chart area values.

Programmatic control

The purpose of providing programmatic control through the Visualization API is to allow the developer to dynamically set chart attributes through various external sources. **Programmatic control** is therefore nothing more than the assignment of available chart attributes through the user interface, or other mechanism capable of triggering an event. Just as the Google Visualization API uses events to enable dynamic activity within itself, JavaScript events such as onclick() or onload() also allow web page events to trigger Visualization API customization.

The following example illustrates the combination of event triggers designed as buttons, which then set visualization option configurations. The buttons are ultimately just presets for the visualized chart. To filter the pie chart to a view of only the 50 to 54 and 55 to 59 years age group ranges, the user would select the **Select 50 to 54 + 55 to 59 years** button.

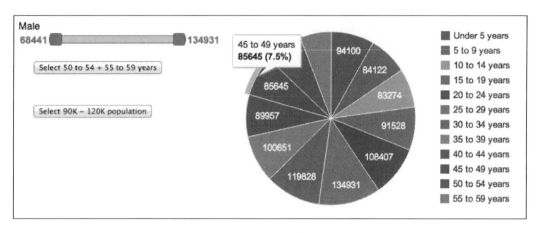

The resulting visualization not only alters the pie chart view, but is also programmed so that the slider configuration changes as well. The button press event is in actuality, linked only to the slider control. In turn, the chart depends on the slider configuration. In this manner, a chain of dependencies is achieved, although the slider can still be manipulated independently of the preset button.

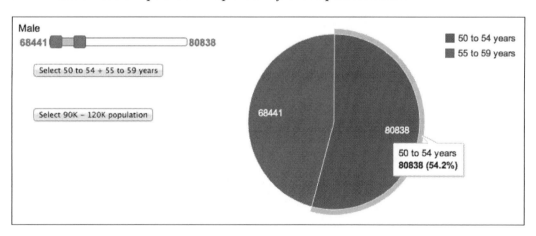

Similarly, when the **Select 90K – 12K population** button is pressed, the slider values are set, which subsequently alters the chart visualization itself.

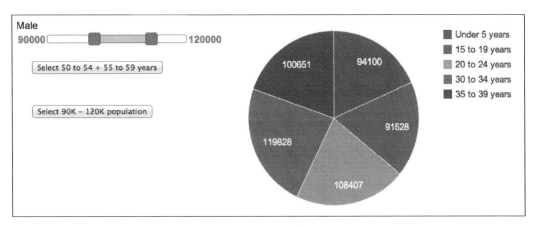

Global variables

To code the preceding example, there is one key difference to recognize as part of creating a programmatic control for a chart. As with previous examples, the function to execute upon triggering the event is organized as a function outside of the main visualization function. The slider and pie chart variables happen to be used in both the functions. However, if these variables are only known to the main visualization function, the execution of the `dashboardReady` code will result in an error when the button event is triggered. This occurrence results in the following **Uncaught ReferenceError: slider is not defined** error message when debugging the code:

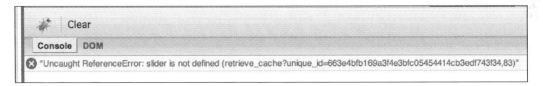

The `slider` in the error is referring to the use of the slider object in the `dashboardReady` function, not the main `drawVisualization` function. The slider object is known to the `drawVisualization` function, but not to the `dashboardReady` function, as they are completely separate functions and `slider` is defined in `drawVisualization` only. To solve this issue and introduce consistency of variables, a variable that is known to the entire scripted application is required. This type of variable is called a **Global variable**. To create a global variable, simply create it outside of either function.

```
<script>

var slider;
varpiechart;

functiondrawVisualization () { … }
…
</script>
```

The declaration of the variable must still be inside the `<script>` tags, but outside of all JavaScript functions in order to be considered global to the application. The slider example declares the global variables, `slider` and `piechart`, at the very beginning of the API script. In this way, both `slider` and `piechart` can be referenced in any function in the API script. The entire HTML code for the programmatic control example is explained by section here. The first section loads the appropriate libraries.

```
<!DOCTYPE html PUBLIC "-//W3C//DTD XHTML 1.0 Strict//EN" "http://www.
w3.org/TR/xhtml1/DTD/xhtml1-strict.dtd">
<html xmlns="http://www.w3.org/1999/xhtml">
  <head>
    <meta http-equiv="content-type" content="text/html;
    charset=utf-8"/>
    <title>
      Google Visualization API Sample
    </title>
    <script type="text/javascript" src="http://www.google.com/
    jsapi"></script>
    <script type="text/javascript">
      google.load('visualization', '1.1', {packages: ['controls']});
    </script>
    <script type="text/javascript">
```

Next, the global `slider` and `piechart` variables are declared. The dataset is created as a `DataTable`, and the `slider` and `piechart` variables are configured.

```
// Define the slider and pie chart variables as global
variables.
var slider;
var piechart;

function drawVisualization() {
  // Prepare the data
  var data = google.visualization.arrayToDataTable([
      ['Age', 'Male'],
      ['Under 5 years',    94100],
      ['5 to 9 years',     84122],
      ['10 to 14 years',   83274],
      ['15 to 19 years',   91528],
      ['20 to 24 years',  108407],
      ['25 to 29 years',  134931],
      ['30 to 34 years',  119828],
      ['35 to 39 years',  100651],
      ['40 to 44 years',   89957],
      ['45 to 49 years',   85645],
      ['50 to 54 years',   80838],
      ['55 to 59 years',   68441]
  ]);

  // Define a slider control for the 'Male Population' column
  slider = new google.visualization.ControlWrapper({
    'controlType': 'NumberRangeFilter',
    'containerId': 'control1',
    'options': {
    'filterColumnLabel': 'Male',
    'ui': {'labelStacking': 'vertical'}
    }
  });

  // Define a pie chart
  piechart = new google.visualization.ChartWrapper({
    'chartType': 'PieChart',
    'containerId': 'chart1',
    'options': {
      'width': 700,
      'height': 400,
      'legend': 'side',
```

```
        'chartArea': {'left': 15, 'top': 15, 'right': 0,
        'bottom': 10},
        'pieSliceText': 'value'
      }
    });
```

At this point, the `dashboard` is defined. Also, the event that listens for the chart to finish rendering is created. The final step is to bind the `slider` and `piechart` controls to the dashboard and draw the chart.

```
// Create the dashboard
var dashboard = new google.visualization.Dashboard(document.
getElementById('dashboard'));

// Register a listener to be notified once the dashboard is ready
to accept presets.
google.visualization.events.addListener(dashboard, 'ready',
dashboardReady);

// Configure the slider to affect the piechart, bind to the
// dashboard
dashboard.bind(slider, piechart).draw(data);


}
```

Outside of the visualization function, the `dashboardReady` function sets the state values for the range slider and preset buttons.

```
function dashboardReady() {
  // The dashboard is ready to accept interaction. Configure the
  buttons to programmatically affect the dashboard when clicked.
  // This button selects the range that happens to be the 50-54 and
  55-59 year age groups
  document.getElementById('rangeButton').onclick = function() {
    slider.setState({'lowValue': 68441, 'highValue': 80838});
    slider.draw();
  };

  // This button selects population numbers between 90K to 120K
  document.getElementById('rangeButton2').onclick = function() {
    slider.setState({'lowValue': 90000, 'highValue': 120000});
    slider.draw();
  };


}
```

The final section of code sets the containers for the slider, buttons, and chart.

```
          google.setOnLoadCallback(drawVisualization);
      </script>
  </head>
  <body style="font-family: Arial;border: 0 none;">
    <div id="dashboard">
<table>
        <tr style='vertical-align: top'>
          <td style='width: 300px; font-size: 0.9em;'>
            <div id="control1"></div>
            <div id="buttons">
              <button style="margin: 2em" id="rangeButton">Select 50
              to 54 + 55 to 59 years</button><br />
              <button style="margin: 2em" id="rangeButton2">Select
              90K - 120K population</button><br />
            </div>
          </td>
          <td style='width: 600px'>
            <div style="float: left;" id="chart1"></div>
          </td>
        </tr>
      </table>
    </div>
  </body>
</html>
```

 Live examples are available at http://gvisapi-packt.
appspot.com/ch7-examples/ch7-progctrl.html.

Dashboards and controls can at first appear to be complicated given the length of code required. However, breaking down the code into functional components reveals the methodical, but simple approach to dashboard construction.

 Dashboard and control documentation is available at https://
developers.google.com/chart/interactive/docs/
gallery/controls.

Transition animation

Sometimes it is helpful to display two sets of data in animated sequence to illustrate the dynamics of the change in data values. The transition animation option in the Visualization API is intended for that purpose.

Controls for triggering a transition animation utilize standard HTML methods. Common elements, such as a simple button-click using the JavaScript `onclick()` method, can be used to initiate animation sequences. The following diagram is of the two states of a visualization. In one state, the total population of Chicago taken in the 2000 Census is shown. In the other state, the 2010 Chicago population is visualized. To toggle between the two bar graphs, the user is provided with a button in the upper-right hand corner of the chart. Pressing the button will toggle the visualization between the 2000 and 2010 population chart. Once the button is pressed, the Visualization API will smoothly transition the bar graph to the selected data representation.

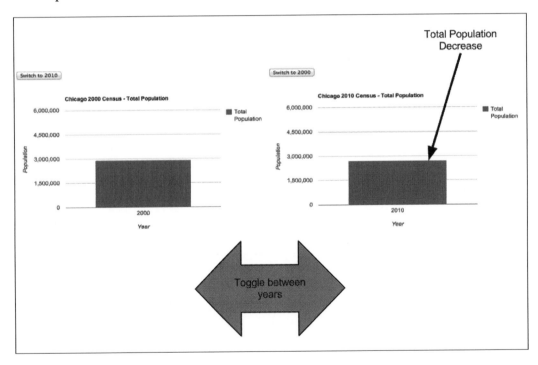

The code for the preceding animation requires both basic HTML and Visualization API methods. The HTML method used in this example is button creation via the `<form>` tag. The behavior of the animation is controlled through Visualization API methods, with the event listener method being particularly useful. At the core, a transition animation must contain the following components:

- A switching method to switch the current dataset being viewed
- A user interface mechanism to trigger the switching between datasets

The animated transition code is as follows, with explanations of these key components afterwards.

```
<!DOCTYPE html>
<html>
  <head>
    <title>Transition Animation Example</title>
  </head>
  <body class="docs framebox_body">

<script type="text/javascript" src="https://www.google.com/jsapi"></
script>

<script type="text/javascript">

google.load('visualization', '1.1', {packages:['corechart']});

google.setOnLoadCallback(total_population);

function total_population() {
   // 2000 and 2010 Chicago Census Data
   var c2000 = [['Year', 'Total Population'],
                  ['2000', 2895964]];
   var c2010 = [['Year', 'Total Population'],
                  ['2010', 2695598]];

   // Create and populate the data tables.
   var data = [];
   data[0] = google.visualization.arrayToDataTable(c2000);
   data[1] = google.visualization.arrayToDataTable(c2010);
   var options = {
```

```
     width: 550,
     height: 350,
     vAxis: {title: "Population"},
     hAxis: {title: "Year"},
     seriesType: "bars",
     animation:{
       duration: 2000,
       easing: 'out'
     }
   };

   // initialize current state
   var current = 0;
     // Create and draw the visualization.
   var chart = new google.visualization.ComboChart(document.
   getElementById('census-visualization'));
   var button = document.getElementById('switch_button');
   function drawChart() {
      // Disabling the button while the chart is drawing.
     button.disabled = true;
     google.visualization.events.addListener(chart, 'ready',
         function() {
           button.disabled = false;
           button.value = 'Switch to ' + (current ? '2000' : '2010');
         });
     options['title'] = 'Chicago ' + (current ? '2010' : '2000') +
     ' Census - Total Population';
     chart.draw(data[current], options);
   }
   drawChart();
   button.onclick = function() {
     current = 1 - current;
     drawChart();
   }
}
</script>
<form><input id="switch_button" type="button" value=""></input></form>
<div id="census-visualization"></div>
</body>
</html>
```

Programmatic switch

Note that in the preceding code, several distinct features are present which are not found in the general use of the Visualization API. For instance, there are two datasets that are kept in a multi-dimensional table, which is an extension of the **array** programming method discussed in *Chapter 4, Basic Charts*.

```
var data = [];
data[0] = google.visualization.arrayToDataTable(c2000);
data[1] = google.visualization.arrayToDataTable(c2010);
```

The preceding technique of creating a collection of tables in a single variable simplifies the job of referencing multiple data tables in a single application. Rather than giving each table a variable name, the tables can easily be referenced by indicating their location in the bigger array. For example, to use the Census dataset from 2000 (c2000), simply use the following notation:

```
data[0]
```

It is also helpful to note where the c2000 variable came from. In the preceding code, c2000 and c2010 are variables that contain the total population for each respective Census year. Instead of referencing c2000 and c2010 individually, the tables are encapsulated into a more manageable, single array denoted as data[]. The nested array is called a **multi-dimensional array**.

> **Best practice**
> Use variables to compact datasets into manageable collections, which are called multi-dimensional arrays.

In practice, the technique of creating switchable arrays is useful when having to toggle between drawings using chart.draw(). In the preceding example, current is the variable that tells the chart which dataset to draw.

```
chart.draw(data[current], options);
```

The next step is to determine how the current variable is set by user clicks, which behaves as a button toggle.

User interface toggle

The current variable selects the dataset to be visualized. The Visualization API does not provide other interface tools other than special use buttons, so an HTML button must be created for the user interface. Still, beyond the HTML creation, all functionality of the button is handled through Visualization API methods.

Create button

The first task is to create an HTML button with an `id` tag, similar to how a visualization requires an `id` for rendering in an HTML framework.

```
<form>
<input id="switch_button" type="button" value=""></input>
</form>
```

In the visualization function, create a variable and assign it to the `<div id>` from the `<form>` section.

```
var button = document.getElementById('switch_button');
```

This creates a direct link from the HTML button to the visualization code. From this point forward, all button behavior that is related to the chart is defined through the Visualization API.

Button behavior

Given that the button is intended to act as a toggle between Census populations, it is desirable to know the initial state of the button. The `current` variable is the behavior trigger for the button. For example, if `current` = `2010`, the population for 2010 will be drawn by the visualization. Ideally, the button text **Switch to 2000/2010** and visualization never become mismatched. There are several best practices to prevent this issue. The first is to initialize the state of the button to a known value when the application starts. To initialize `current`, it is assigned an initial value of 0.

```
// initialize current state
var current = 0;
```

To prevent mismatched states between the button text and visualized data, the use of a single variable to set the state of the visualization and the button is suggested.

```
button.value = 'Switch to ' + (current ? '2000' : '2010');
  });
```

Note the title is set with the same method so as to keep labeling current for the chart.

```
options['title'] = 'Chicago' + (current ? '2010' : '2000') + ' Census
- Total Population';
```

You also have to control button pushes while the chart is drawing. When it is done drawing, it will send out a ready message. An event listener for this message lets the application know when it is ok to accept another button push.

```
// Disabling the button while the chart is drawing.
 button.disabled = true;
google.visualization.events.addListener(chart, 'ready',
     function() {
       button.disabled = false;
```

Best practice

As is the case with programming in general, avoid bugs by properly managing variables. For variables that hold a state, initialize them when the application starts. To prevent mismatched states, try to use only one "variable of truth" to set multiple aspects of the visualization.

Another example of the transition advantages can be viewed when the 2000 and 2010 Census data are placed side by side for one sex. The transition illustrates the difference in growth (or decline) for each of the sexes during each of the Census years.

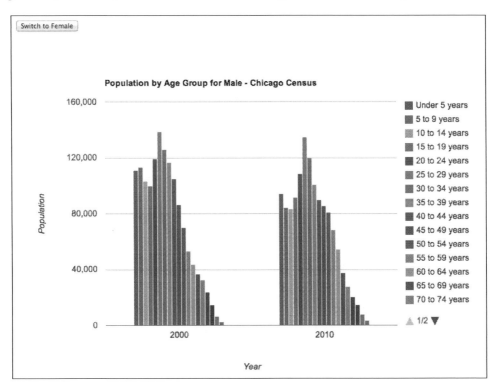

Live examples are available at `http://gvisapi-packt.`
`appspot.com/ch7-examples/ch7-transanimate0.html`.
`http://gvisapi-packt.appspot.com/ch7-examples/ch7-`
`transanimate.html`

For the preceding example, the data may be more detailed, but the framework design for the animation remains the same.

 Chart transition animation documentation is available at `https://developers.google.com/chart/interactive/docs/animation`.

Chart editor for users

The chart editor, as seen in Spreadsheet visualizations, can become part of a coded visualization. With the chart editor option, users can set their own style and chart type preferences. The editor is the same editor used by Spreadsheets and Fusion Tables. To make chart editor an option, a button to open the editor must be created in the standard HTML form method.

```
<input type='button' onclick='openEditor()' value='Open Editor'>
```

The remaining methods to implement the editor are primarily the same as with other button-controlled charts.

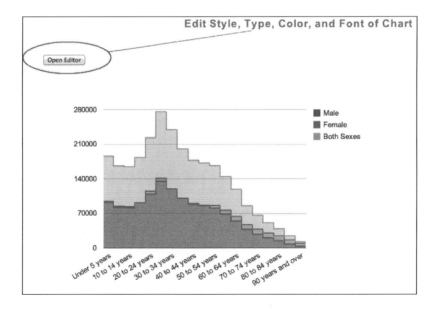

However, one small programming requirement in addition to the editor-specific button itself, is to include the `chartedit` library package to be loaded by `google.load`.

```
google.load('visualization', '1', {packages:['charteditor']});
```

To create the chart itself, the `ChartWrapper` class is used. Finally, to alert the application when the editor button has been pushed, an event listener is used. The creation of the listener is in the same form as other event handlers. The listener is created with the `addListener` code, and is encapsulated in its own function, `openEditor()`.Since the **Open Editor** button has been defined as equal to `'openEditor()'` and its `onclick` event in the `<body>` tag, pressing the **Open Editor** button will trigger `addListener` to execute the `openEditor()` function.

```
function openEditor() {
  // Handler for the "Open Editor" button.
  var editor = new google.visualization.ChartEditor();
  google.visualization.events.addListener(editor, 'ok',
    function() {
      wrapper = editor.getChartWrapper();
      wrapper.draw(document.getElementById('visualization'));
    });
  editor.openDialog(wrapper);
}
```

The following is the complete HTML for a chart with editor capabilities. The data for this example is imported from a Google Spreadsheet.

```
<!DOCTYPE html PUBLIC "-//W3C//DTD XHTML 1.0 Strict//EN" "http://www.
w3.org/TR/xhtml1/DTD/xhtml1-strict.dtd">
<html xmlns="http://www.w3.org/1999/xhtml">
  <head>
    <meta http-equiv="content-type" content="text/html;
    charset=utf-8"/>
    <title>
      Google Visualization with Editor
    </title>
    <script type="text/javascript" src="http://www.google.com/
    jsapi"></script>
    <script type="text/javascript">
      google.load('visualization', '1', {packages: ['charteditor']});
    </script>
    <script type="text/javascript">
    var wrapper;

      //Use ChartWrapper to create chart
    function init() {
```

```
    wrapper = new google.visualization.ChartWrapper({
      dataSourceUrl: 'https://docs.google.com/spreadsheet/tq?key=0Ah
      nmGz1SteeGdEVsNlNWWkoxU3ZRQjlmbDdTTjF2dHc&range=A1%3AD20&head
      ers=-1',
      containerId: 'visualization',
      chartType: 'SteppedAreaChart'
    });
    wrapper.draw();
  }

  function openEditor() {
    // Handler for the "Open Editor" button.
    var editor = new google.visualization.ChartEditor();
    google.visualization.events.addListener(editor, 'ok',
      function() {
        wrapper = editor.getChartWrapper();
        wrapper.draw(document.getElementById('visualization'));
      });
    editor.openDialog(wrapper);
  }


  google.setOnLoadCallback(init);

  </script>
 </head>
 <body style="font-family: Arial;border: 0 none;">
   <input type='button' onclick='openEditor()' value='Open Editor'>
   <div id='visualization' style="width:600px;height:400px">
 </body>
</html>
```

You can have a look at the live example at http://gvisapi-packt.
appspot.com/ch7-examples/ch7-editor.html.

You will have the chart editor documentation at https://
developers.google.com/chart/interactive/docs/
reference#google_visualization_charteditor.

Summary

Beyond chart creation, the Google Visualization API provides methods for user interaction. Data presented in a chart may be configured to allow a user to manipulate views, ranges, and even styles of the chart itself. Visualizations may also be presented in various sequences, with transition animation to illustrate the change in data values. In this chapter, visualization customization is focused on pre-defined controls used as enhancements to fairly basic charts. Similarly, animation and editor capabilities are somewhat static with controls being added to enhance user experience. In the next chapter, advanced visualization customization and complex methods of chart creation are introduced. Topics are expanded to charts able to interactively display additional data dimensions. Additionally, the first steps to developing a custom visualization from scratch are introduced.

8
Advanced Charts

This chapter covers several advanced topics concerning the Google Visualization API. Some examples may have multiple approaches, while others are bound to a specific method. In fact, more than one of the complex charts presented can also be created using either spreadsheets or code. Although the charts themselves may require very little code, they do require various types of data to be formatted as per specifications. Additionally, advanced charts often require a handful of settings to be configured in order to render the chart drawing at all. Good examples of chart requiring particular care with data organization are time-based charts and intensity maps. Often these types of charts appear complex, but most of the complexity has been encapsulated in the visualization code itself. The result is then a collection of interconnected configuration requirements. The interplay between more complex requirements and increasingly advanced charts is the topic of the final section of this chapter, *Your own visualization*.

In this chapter we will cover the following topics:

- Time-based charts
- Intensity/marker maps
- Writing your own visualization

Time-based charts

When data value is dependent on the passing of time, a representation of the element of time must be included in the visualization. Time-based charts are the charts that animate a change in data values over a time period. Through this animation, the chart is able to graphically represent movement in values over time.

There are several time-reliant charts available through the Google Visualization API. At this time, they are the motion chart and the annotated timeline chart.

Motion chart

A **motion chart** is a visualization that animates the change in data over time. The data representation and animation of this chart can be displayed as three different chart types, bubble, bar, and line. The Size of the data point bubbles can also be set to represent additional data attributes. Colors, highlighted items, and motion tracking are also available as user control options on the chart.

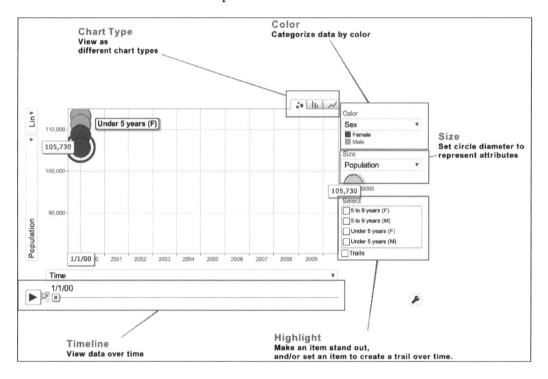

Possibly the most important control of the Motion Chart is the ▶ button.

This button is self-explanatory in that the graphic on it is recognizable as a generic "play" button. It is intended to set the chart in motion and also pause it. Directly to the right of the "play" button is the motion speed control. The speed at which the animation progresses is controlled by the smaller arrow set on top of a column of horizontal lines. Dragging this control upwards or downwards dynamically changes the animation speed.

The **Color** setting on the motion chart example is configured to display blue for female and lime green for the male age groups. Selecting the tab below the **Color** label allows the user to change the color setting to several other options. These options include a default where all bubbles are of the same color, reliant on a data column, or the same color for all items. As additional columns are added to the dataset, they will become available as a variable in the **Color** drop-down menu.

You can find the **Size** setting just below **Color**. This setting determines the diameter of the motion bubbles, and can be configured to reflect a number value associated with a category or item. In this example, the diameter of the dots is related to the sizes of the 2000 and 2010 populations of male and female age groups in Chicago.

The **Select** setting is used to highlight one or more of the data category dots on the graph. Selected dots will appear solid in opacity, whereas unselected dots are opaque.

After the chart has been set into motion, the current point in time for the chart is available along the bottom of the chart.

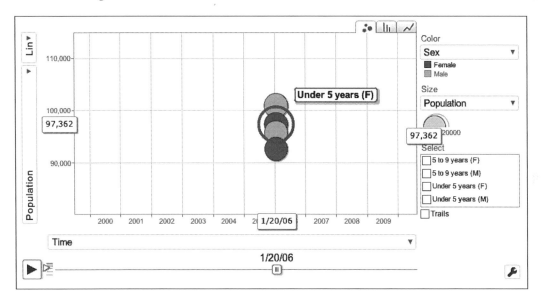

When the data has completed displaying the timeline's data, the data circles will come to a stop at the end of the graph.

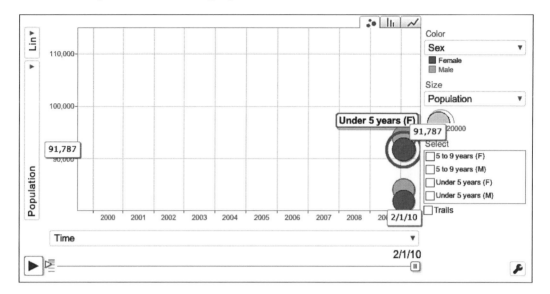

The motion chart offers two other types of charts to view animated data. The second tab shows data as an animated bar chart. The timeline player functions the same in this version, with bars changing in height.

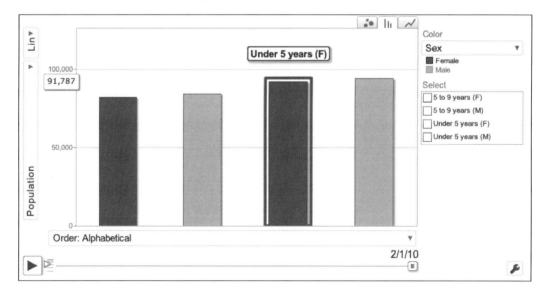

Depending on the order of the data in the data source, the bars of the chart may switch places graphically as one value becomes higher than another. To prevent this behavior, select the down arrow to change the **Order** option of the horizontal axis. Generally the switching behavior occurs when **Alphabetical** is the selected order.

The third type of viewing available is a simple line graph. This view is not animated, but a static representation of the data.

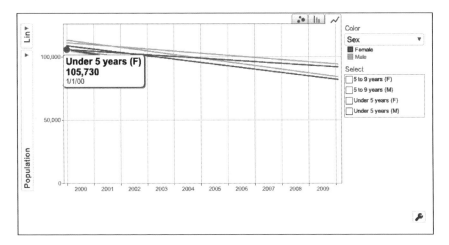

Another useful feature available on the motion chart user interface is the **Trails** option. When this option is selected, the chart draws a trail behind the data point as it traverses the graph over time. This feature is useful for examining the paths of a data point in relation to other data points as they move through time.

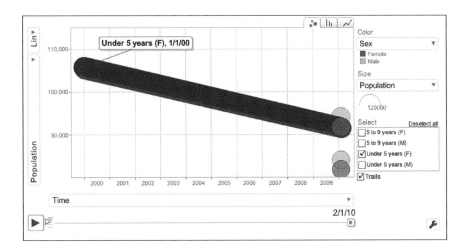

Finally, a small but useful display control option on a motion chart is the linear or logarithmic toggle. Found in the left-right corner of the chart, this control allows the viewer to change how the animation is interpreted between values. Selecting the **Log** option prepares the chart for the data values according to logarithmic scale. Alternatively, selecting the **Lin** option sets the data scale to linear.

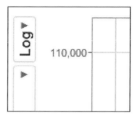

Spreadsheets

Inserting a motion chart into a Google Spreadsheet is as simple as selecting **Insert | Chart** from the spreadsheet menu bar. The Chart Editor lists the options for visualizations, with the motion chart being categorized under **Trend**. As with all other Google Spreadsheet charts, the organization of data in the spreadsheet is extremely important.

The first column should contain the names of the items to be tracked on the chart. The second column consists of the sequence of dates the timeline will contain. The remaining columns can be either text or number values. In our example, the age groups of the 2000 and 2010 Chicago Census population transition from their 2000 and 2010 values.

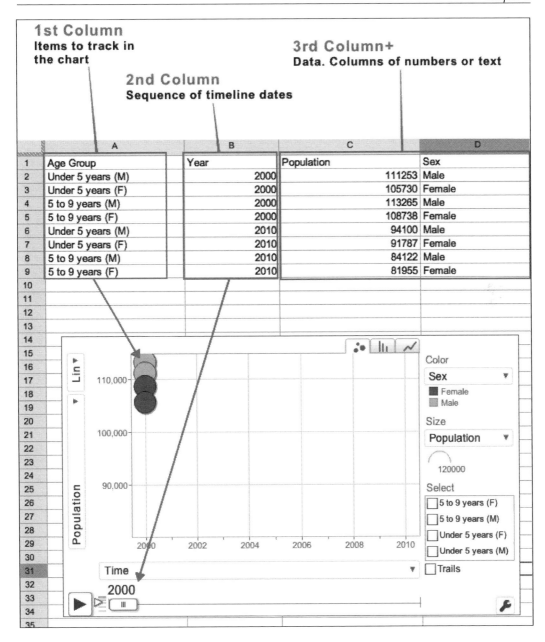

Data for the United States Census 2000 can be found at `http://www.factfinder2.census.gov`. From this page, search for the desired region, which in this case is Chicago, Illinois.

The live example is available at `https://docs.google.com/` `spreadsheet/ccc?key=0AhnmGz1SteeGdHlKQUJzWmxWdj` `Z5NjhORDBSMnpZVFE`.

Code

The same motion chart created in Spreadsheets can also be realized using Google Visualization API code.

As with other charts, the same process of creating a chart from the library package load to the end visualization consists of several key components:

- **Loading the appropriate library**:

```
google.load('visualization', '1', {packages:['motionchart']});
```

- **Creating or loading data into a** `DataTable()` **method**:

```
var data = new google.visualization.DataTable();
```

- **Drawing the chart**:

```
var motionchart = new google.visualization.MotionChart();
```

The only noticeable difference between any basic visualization and a motion chart visualization is the inclusion of a `date` column. When describing a date for the Google Visualization API, the following format must be used:

```
new date(year, day, month)
```

The API will then interpret the column of dates and display them as points on the timeline. The complete code for the Motion Chart visualization is as follows:

```
<!DOCTYPE html PUBLIC "-//W3C//DTD XHTML 1.0 Strict//EN" "http://www.
w3.org/TR/xhtml1/DTD/xhtml1-strict.dtd">
<html xmlns="http://www.w3.org/1999/xhtml">
<head>
  <meta http-equiv="content-type" content="text/html;
  charset=utf-8" />
  <title>Google Visualization API Sample</title>
  <script type="text/javascript"
  src="http://www.google.com/jsapi"></script>

  <script type="text/javascript">
    google.load('visualization', '1',
    {packages: ['motionchart']});

    function drawVisualization() {
```

```
var data = new google.visualization.DataTable();
data.addColumn('string', 'Age Group');
data.addColumn('date', 'Date');
data.addColumn('number', 'Population');
data.addColumn('string', 'Sex');
data.addRows([
  ['Under 5 years (M)', new Date(2000,0,1), 111253, 'Male'],
  ['Under 5 years (F)', new Date(2000,0,1),
  105730, 'Female'],
  ['5 to 9 years (M)', new Date(2000,0,1), 113265, 'Male'],
  ['5 to 9 years (F)', new Date(2000,0,1),
  108738, 'Female'],
  ['Under 5 years (M)', new Date(2010,1,1), 94100, 'Male'],
  ['Under 5 years (F)', new Date(2010,1,1),
  91787, 'Female'],
  ['5 to 9 years (M)', new Date(2010,1,1), 84122, 'Male'],
  ['5 to 9 years (F)', new Date(2010,1,1), 81955, 'Female']

]);
var motionchart = new google.visualization.MotionChart(
  document.getElementById('visualization'));
  motionchart.draw(data, {'width': 800, 'height': 400});
}


  google.setOnLoadCallback(drawVisualization);
</script>
</head>
<body style="font-family: Arial;border: 0 none;">
<div id="visualization" style="width: 800px; height: 400px;"></div>
</body>
</html>
```

> The live example is avaialable at http://gvisapi-packt.
> appspot.com/ch8-examples/ch8-motion.html.

Additional information regarding motion charts can be found on the Google
Developers website.

> The Motion Chart documentation is available at https://developers.
> google.com/chart/interactive/docs/gallery/motionchart.

The lesson to be learned from motion charts is primarily how to manage time-based data. It is also worth noting that the code implementation of the motion chart is similar to basic charts, with only a few minor adjustments. The motion chart itself is a complex visualization, with many possible input and output variations. The reduction of complexity for developers using a visualization in their code is a desirable outcome when developing custom visualization types. This is especially true for visualizations that are easy to implement, but provide many options to developers or users as to the configuration and formatting of their data set.

Annotated timeline

The **annotated timeline** provides the ability to zoom in or out on a set of data, in addition to tagging specific points with additional descriptions. The annotated timeline is available in Spreadsheets as well as in code form.

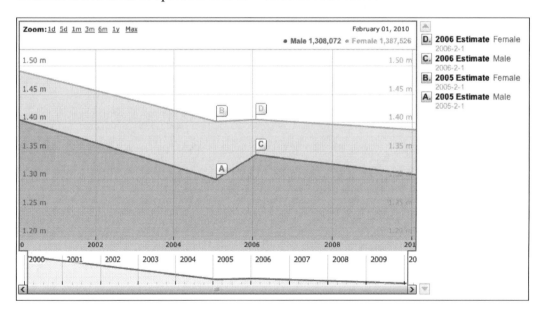

Data source: `factfinder2.census.gov`

This chart requires limited amounts of data to create, but has the ability to include a significant amount of description data as well. Unlike the motion chart, the annotated timeline chart gives the user a zoom feature through the ability to focus on specific segments of the overall timeline using the adjustable window along the bottom of the chart. In addition to zooming capabilities, it is possible to flag specific data points and give these points additional descriptive values.

In the preceding example, the total populations of males and females in the various Census for actual and estimate years between 2000 and 2010 are visualized. With the estimates included, it is possible to see the decrease in population over the 10-year period was not linear. The 2005 and 2006 estimate values for both male and female populations have also been graphed and noted. The notations help provide insight for changes in the linearity of the population decline.

Spreadsheets

Visualizing an annotated timeline in Google Spreadsheets follows the same procedure as motion charts. The package (`annotated timeline`) is loaded, data is put into a `DataTable()`, and the visualization is drawn. However, there is a small but distinct difference between other charts and the annotated timeline in the particular importance of empty data fields.

Event flags and descriptions

For annotated timeline charts, blank (or null) values in the data set are just as important as other data. The formatting for this type of chart starts with the first column containing timeline dates. The second column contains data values to be displayed, with the third and fourth columns being the event flag title and descriptions.

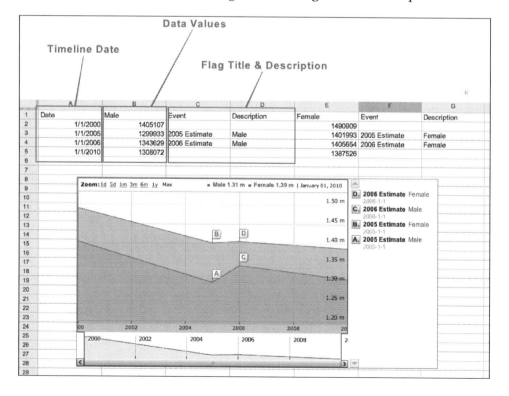

For data points that do not have associated event flags, the cell is left empty. Additionally, if more than one category of data is to be displayed, the column patterns of data values, event flags, and title descriptions are repeated as necessary after the first set. As this is true with individual event flag information, if a flag or description is not needed at a specific data point, the corresponding cells are left empty.

 The live example is available at https://docs.google.com/ spreadsheet/ccc?key=0AhnmGz1SteeGdHN0Qi1NeUo5UlZ KVnVkcEFEeUtpZUE.

Code

The coded version of the annotated timeline is very similar to other visualizations, with a minor change required in how data is passed or defined in DataTable(). For annotated timelines, data values that do not require an event tag or description must be filled with the value null in the DataTable().

```
var data = new google.visualization.DataTable();
  data.addColumn('date', 'Date');
  data.addColumn('number', 'Male');
  data.addColumn('string', 'Event');
  data.addColumn('string', 'Description');
  data.addColumn('number', 'Female');
  data.addColumn('string', 'Event');
  data.addColumn('string', 'Description');
  data.addRows([

  [new Date(2000, 1 ,1), 1405107,
  null, null, 1490909, null, null],
  [new Date(2005, 1 ,1), 1299933,
  '2005 Estimate', 'Male', 1401993, '2005 Estimate', 'Female'],
  [new Date(2006, 1 ,1), 1343629,
  '2006 Estimate', 'Male', 1405654, '2006 Estimate', 'Female'],
  [new Date(2010, 1 ,1), 1308072,
  null, null, 1387526, null, null]
  ]);
```

Notice that the previous table is constructed in the same manner as other tables, with empty values of the array being replaced with null.

The following code is entirely an annotated timeline example. Optional settings, such as maximum, minimum, opacity, and colors are configured with the `options` array. In the Spreadsheet form, these are the configurations that can be found under **Customize Tab** in the Chart Editor:

```
<!DOCTYPE html PUBLIC "-//W3C//DTD XHTML 1.0 Strict//EN" "http://www.
w3.org/TR/xhtml1/DTD/xhtml1-strict.dtd">
<html xmlns="http://www.w3.org/1999/xhtml">
<head>
  <meta http-equiv="content-type" content="text/html;
  charset=utf-8" />
  <title>Google Visualization API Sample</title>
  <script type="text/javascript"
  src="http://www.google.com/jsapi"></script>
  <script type="text/javascript">
    google.load('visualization', '1',
    {packages: ['annotatedtimeline']});
    function drawVisualization() {
      var data = new google.visualization.DataTable();
      data.addColumn('date', 'Date');
      data.addColumn('number', 'Male');
      data.addColumn('string', 'Event');
      data.addColumn('string', 'Description');
      data.addColumn('number', 'Female');
      data.addColumn('string', 'Event');
      data.addColumn('string', 'Description');
      data.addRows([
        [new Date(2000, 1 ,1), 1405107, null, null,
        1490909, null, null],
        [new Date(2005, 1 ,1), 1299933, '2005 Estimate', 'Male',
        1401993, '2005 Estimate', 'Female'],
        [new Date(2006, 1 ,1), 1343629, '2006 Estimate', 'Male',
        1405654, '2006 Estimate', 'Female'],
        [new Date(2010, 1 ,1), 1308072, null, null,
        1387526, null, null]
      ]);

    var annotatedtimeline = new
    google.visualization.AnnotatedTimeLine(
      document.getElementById('visualization'));
    annotatedtimeline.draw(data, {
      'colors': ['green', 'orange'], // The colors to be used
      'displayAnnotations': true,
      'displayExactValues': true, // Do not truncate values
```

```
          'displayRangeSelector' : true, // Show the range selector
          'displayZoomButtons': true, // Display the zoom buttons
          'fill': 30, // Fill area below the lines with 20% opacity
          'legendPosition': 'newRow', // Can be sameRow
          'max': 1500000, // Override the automatic default
          'min': 1200000, // Override the automatic default
          'scaleColumns': [0, 1], // 2 scales, by 1st& 2nd lines
          'scaleType': 'allmaximized', // Fixed or maximized.
          'thickness': 2, // Make the lines thicker
          'zoomStartTime': new Date(2000, 1 ,1),
          'zoomEndTime': new Date(2010, 1 ,1)
        });
      }

    google.setOnLoadCallback(drawVisualization);
  </script>
</head>
<body style="font-family: Arial;border: 0 none;">
<div id="visualization" style="width: 800px; height: 400px;"></div>
</body>
</html>
```

Here's an important pointer to take care of.

Make sure the ranges of cells in view are as expected as you add, delete or reorganize the spreadsheet.

The annotated timeline is most useful when a series of time-related data points require occasional notation at various instances. As demonstrated in the example code, the annotated timeline also allows for a reasonable amount of customization in the format.

The live example is available at `http://gvisapi-packt.appspot.com/ch8-examples/ch8-timeline.html`.

Additional information regarding annotated timelines can be found on the Google Developers website.

The annotated timeline documentation is available at `https://developers.google.com/chart/interactive/docs/gallery/annotatedtimeline`.

Maps

For any data that can be tied to a geographic location, map visualizations are often very desirable. However, unlike simple bar graphs and line charts, it would be very difficult to redraw entire geographic regions of the world every time a visualization were needed. So, it would seem a basic template of geographic regions at varying scope would be helpful for developers. Rather than requiring all map visualizations to be created with the Google Maps API, the Visualization API provides several basic geographic data maps. These basic charts are the `geochart` and `geomap` visualizations. Both `geomap` and `geochart` are methods of representing intensity or quantity across geographical spaces, from provinces or states to worldwide.

geochart versus geomap

The only key difference between `geomap` and `geochart` visualizations is the method used to render the actual drawing of the map. Any other differences stem from the difference in rendering techniques. `geomap` uses Adobe Flash, which is quick to implement but lacks certain configuration options. `geochart` is rendered in **VML (Vector Markup Language)** or **SVG (Scalable Vector Graphics)**, which allows for more detailed configurations. Finally, `geochart` (but not `geomap`) is also available as a chart option in Google Spreadsheets. These differences are generally due to the fact that `geochart` is the newer version although `geomap` has not yet been depreciated. Regardless, HTML5 or CSS3 `geochart` is the preferred choice over the older Flash version.

The frameworks of both `geochart` and `geomap` are also very similar to each other. Both visualizations have two modes of display, `regions` and `markers`. (The `auto` setting will select which of the two is the best fit for the data.) The `regions` setting displays data associated with cities, states, or countries as a color gradient in the shape of the state. The selection of the color for each state or country is determined by the value of the associated data. In the following example, higher data numbers correspond to darker blue states, while lighter blue indicates lower numbers.

The region option

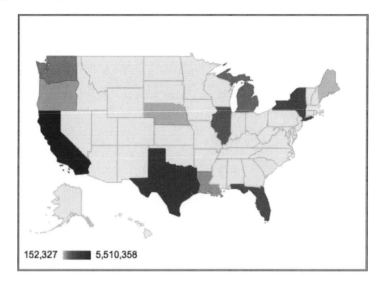

The `marker` mode displays the same quantitative data as the `region` option. However, quantity is visualized through the diameter of each marker point in addition to data-related color variations. For a `geochart` with a number of marker points in a small geographical area, enable the `magnifyingGlass` option as part of the `draw` method's options.

The marker option

Both the region and marker versions of the map are interactive. Hovering over an item on either chart will activate a pop-up window with detailed information.

geochart

Basic `geochart` data formatting consists of two columns. The first column lists geographical locations and the second associates a data value with the corresponding location in each row. In the column of locations, each location should be of the same type. For example, United States and France are countries and are thus of the same type. A mismatch of type would be a data column that lists North America and Mexico City, as one is a continent and the other is a city. To define the geographic scope of a `geochart`, there are several configuration requirements that must be set.

Setting requirements for `geochart`:

- Define a region
- Define a resolution

The `region` option will set the overall scope for the map. Regions are the larger of the two settings, and will have a value of world, or a specific continent, country, state, or province as identified by the ISO 3166 global naming standard. The `resolution` setting then defines the granularity of the specified region. The available options for the `resolution` setting are countries, provinces, or metros. Note that, depending on the region selected, certain options may not be available as resolutions. However, resolutions follow the same ISO 3166 global naming standard as regions.

 Resolution options may vary depending on the region selected.

The ISO 3166 standard

ISO 3166 is an internationally standardized list that defines two or three digit codes for countries, territories, and other subdivisions around the world. The ISO 3166 is published and maintained by the **International Standards Organization (ISO)**. The Google Visualization API complies with this standard when specifying the scope and granularity of geographic areas.

Spreadsheets

The geochart visualization is available as a chart option in the Google Spreadsheets Chart Editor. To use geochart, the first column in the spreadsheet must contain geographical information, such as the names of countries or states. The second column must contain numerical values related to the geographic names listed in the first column.

geochart in Spreadsheets – limitation

The Spreadsheets version of geochart only allows for a single column of data (beyond the region column). To use more columns in the visualization, create geochart using the code method.

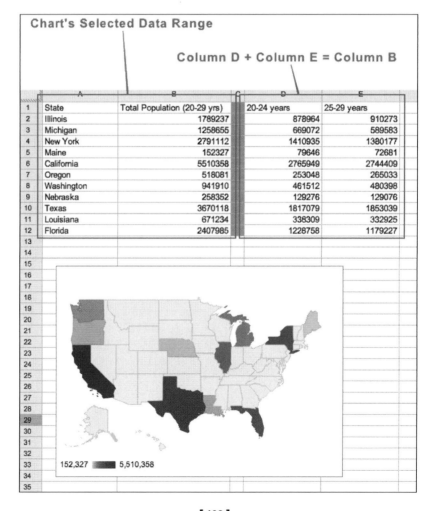

Chart's Selected Data Range

Column D + Column E = Column B

	A	B	C	D	E
1	State	Total Population (20-29 yrs)		20-24 years	25-29 years
2	Illinois	1789237		878964	910273
3	Michigan	1258655		669072	589583
4	New York	2791112		1410935	1380177
5	Maine	152327		79646	72681
6	California	5510358		2765949	2744409
7	Oregon	518081		253048	265033
8	Washington	941910		461512	480398
9	Nebraska	258352		129276	129076
10	Texas	3670118		1817079	1853039
11	Louisiana	671234		338309	332925
12	Florida	2407985		1228758	1179227

152,327 ▬▬ 5,510,358

Source: `factfinder2.census.gov`

In the preceding example, the second column holds the combined population of two familiar Chicago Census age groups, 20-24 years and 25-29 years. The additional functionality of the spreadsheet is used here to convert raw numbers into the desired values to be displayed. In this case, the desired metric is the total population of people between ages 20 and 30 years who reside in a selected group of U.S. The chart range is set to only visualize the first two columns, which results in the visualization of the combination of the raw values.

Code

The overall framework for `geochart` is not much different from other chart frameworks. The only difference is the required configuration of the `region` and `resolution` options as seen in the Chart Editor of the Spreadsheet version.

```
// Set to: auto / regions / markers
displayMode: 'regions',

// Set to: countries / provinces / metros
resolution: 'provinces',
```

The following code snippet is the complete example of `geochart`:

```
<html xmlns="http://www.w3.org/1999/xhtml">
<head>
  <meta http-equiv="content-type" content="text/html;
  charset=utf-8" />
  <title>Google Visualization API Sample</title>
  <script type="text/javascript"
  src="http://www.google.com/jsapi"></script>
  <script type="text/javascript">
    google.load('visualization', '1', {packages: ['geochart']});

    function drawVisualization() {
      // Import data from the Spreadsheets example of Geochart
      var query = new google.visualization.Query(
      'https://docs.google.com/spreadsheet/
      pub?key=0AhnmGz1SteeGdHFQOUx5amozd1NxeGM4MXhwQ1BMdGc&single=
      true&gid=0&range=Sheet1!A2%3AB12&output=html');

      // Send the query with a callback function.
      query.send(handleQueryResponse);
```

```
      }

      // Query handling for the Spreadsheet data
      function handleQueryResponse(response) {
        if (response.isError()) {
          alert('Error in query: ' + response.getMessage() + ' ' +
          response.getDetailedMessage());
          return;
        }
        // Put the data from the Spreadsheet in the 'data' variable
        var data = response.getDataTable();

        options = {region: 'US',
        displayMode: 'regions',
        // Note 'provinces' means states for USA
        resolution: 'provinces',
        // Set color gradient
        colorAxis: {colors: ['#ADC2EB','#000046']},
        width: 556, height: 347,
        // Set mouseover tooltip color
        tooltip: {textStyle: {color: '#FF6633'},
        showColorCode: true},
        };

      var geochart = new google.visualization.GeoChart(
        document.getElementById('visualization'));

        geochart.draw(data, options);
      }

    google.setOnLoadCallback(drawVisualization);
  </script>
</head>
<body style="font-family: Arial;border: 0 none;">
<div id="visualization"></div>
</body>
</html>
```

geomap

As the predecessor to `geochart`, `geomap` inherently has fewer opportunities for customization. This is largely due to the fact that the graphic rendering process is handled by Adobe Flash. The `geomap` visualization, however, has its usages. For example, as a Flash file, `geomap` is compatible with any browser that supports Flash. If for some reason a browser does not support or has trouble reconciling VML or SVG, the visualization cannot run. The Flash format also requires fewer variables to be set, as the `resolution` variable is automatically configured based on the `region` setting.

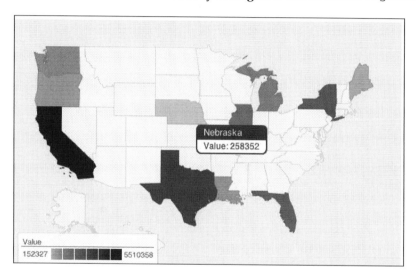

The following screenshot shows the `geomap` visualization in the `marker` mode:

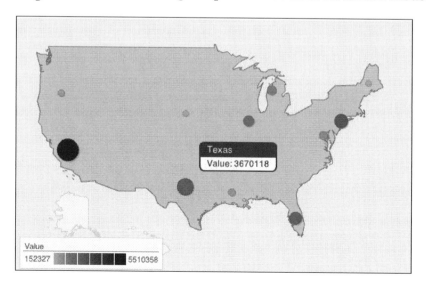

Code

The code for a `geomap` visualization is very similar to the `geochart`. In fact, the only difference between the two types is the visualization name and formatting of the options.

```
var options = {
  dataMode: 'markers', region: 'US',
  colors: ['0xADC2EB','0x000046']
};
  var geomap = new google.visualization.GeoMap(
  document.getElementById('visualization'));
  geomap.draw(data, options);
```

Given that `geomap` is considered as the earlier version of `geochart`, it would come as no surprise if Google decided to depreciate the older `geomap`. Also, the inclusion of `geochart` and not `geomap` in Spreadsheets indicates a possible slow depreciation to come for `geomap`.

> Google technology and tools are constantly improving and changing. Often this means a product has come to the end of its life and is no longer developed. Another possibility is for a tool or feature to be combined with other Google products. To keep abreast of changes, there is really one general rule of thumb to follow when evaluating the lifespan of a Google technology.

From this observation the following question arises: Is the tool or technology being actively integrated with key Google products?

> It's true; the documentation is not being regularly updated or even the word "depreciated" is appearing in the documentation, but it seems a tool or technology is expected to be around for a while if it is actively being integrated with stable Google offerings. Regardless, it is still wise to regularly check the status of tools, technology, or applications provided by Google, especially if they are in a beta phase.
>
> A live example of `geochart` is available at http://gvisapi-packt.appspot.com/ch8-examples/ch8-geochart.html.
>
> A live example of `geomap` is available at http://gvisapi-packt.appspot.com/ch8-examples/ch8-geomap.html.

For more information on geomap, geochart, ISO 3166, and the aforementioned graphics standard, visit the following links:

- geomap **visualization**: https://developers.google.com/chart/interactive/docs/gallery/geomap

- geochart **visualization**: https://developers.google.com/chart/interactive/docs/gallery/geochart

- **Scalable Vector Graphics (SVG)**: http://www.w3.org/Graphics/SVG/

- **Vector Markup Language (VML)**: http://www.w3.org/TR/NOTE-VML

- **ISO 3166 Documentation**: http://www.iso.org/iso/home/standards/country_codes.htm

Map API

geochart and geomap are not intended to be overly sophisticated visualizations, and do not therefore provide the detail of control available in the Google Map API. In the Map API, layers are introduced as a method for creating heat maps, outlined areas, elevation visualizations, overlays, and other data-rich options for maps. An in-depth exploration of the Map API is out of the scope of this book, but it is mentioned here to highlight the importance of knowing the strengths and weaknesses between similar functionality in different APIs. The Visualization API can also be thought of as a jumping off point for learning the Maps API, as frameworks' elements such as getID, listeners, button on-click messages, and other features are often the same between the Google APIs.

The Map API documentation is available at https://developers.google.com/maps/.

Your own visualization

In many ways, authoring a custom visualization is out of the scope of this book. However, it is worthwhile to be aware of the basic steps required to create a visualization from scratch, just in case a requirement for such a chart arises in the future. The general method of creating new visualizations involves knowledge of the HTML **DOM (Document Object Model)** and a reasonable amount of comfort working with programming abstraction.

To start, it is best to know some basic terminology that will be encountered when attempting to build a custom chart. As mentioned in *Chapter 4*, *Basic Charts*, the Google Visualization API is structured as an inheritance-based model. Classes of functions are realized through programming instances. The Visualization API charts, for example, `barchart`, `geochart`, `areachart`, and so on, become instances of a bundle of code when they are used in a program. In programming, the creation of an instance is taken care of by an element of code called the **constructor**. In order to build a custom visualization, a constructor, as well as a draw method of the chart must be defined. To build these elements and then translate them into something that an HTML page can understand, the HTML DOM is used. The HTML DOM is an agreed-upon standard for programmatically retrieving, modifying, adding, and deleting HTML elements.

At its simplest definition, a visualization chart is nothing more than a method for telling the HTML page what to do. The API is then just pre-configured with HTML-compatible rules for drawing graphics from data, which are given to the Chart app.

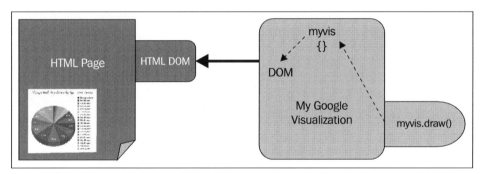

This section is not intended as an in-depth tutorial for HTML DOM object writing. It simply discusses the framework that can be used to manipulate the HTML DOM and encapsulate the functionality as a Google Visualization. This section discusses the ability to create custom chart types.

 The custom visualization documentation is available at https:// developers.google.com/chart/interactive/docs/dev/. JavaScript and HTML DOM references are available at http:// www.w3schools.com/jsref/default.asp.

Building custom visualizations requires additional expertise with the JavaScript HTML DOM. W3Schools provides a nice introduction to working with the DOM.

 JavaScript and HTML DOM examples are available at `http://www.w3schools.com/js/js_ex_dom.asp`.

A custom visualization example is available at `http://gvisapi-packt.appspot.com/ch8-examples/ch8-custom.html`.

Summary

Continuing to create basic and experimental visualizations using the Google Chart API will increase a developer's ability to use the toolset in new and creative ways. As demonstrated in this chapter, the complexity of a visualization may be deceiving in regards to the expertise needed to implement. Often it is the case that visualization complexity has been intentionally encapsulated within the visualization object itself, allowing developers the luxury of less programming during implementation.

Building visualizations from scratch is beyond the scope of this book, but an overview of the process has been presented as a starting point. This book, in combination with the live tutorials, gives a basic foundation of a single API from which advanced use of this API or exploration of other Google APIs can begin. In the next chapter, the various ways in which a visualization can be published are examined.

9
Publishing Options

An advantageous feature of applications written with the Google Visualization API is the diversity of publishing options. Visualizations can be published as an integrated part of a Spreadsheet or Fusion Tables application or, at the other extreme, as a standalone web application. Being scripted applications, Visualization API apps can go just about anywhere HTML can go.

In this chapter we will cover:

- Sharing with Google
- Publishing from Spreadsheets and Fusion Tables
- Embedding in web pages (including App Engine apps)

It is worth noting at this time that Google Gadgets have not been included in this chapter as an option for publishing visualizations. At the time of this book's publication the future support of gadgets was unclear, with several Google applications depreciating their support of gadgets. That being said, Google Gadgets itself is a publishing option but will not be discussed in detail in this chapter. For more information on the topic of gadgets, informative links are provided at the end of the chapter.

Sharing

For visualizations integrated into Spreadsheets or Fusion Tables, it is possible to share work with others by using the built-in Google Apps file sharing method. With Google file sharing, visualizations can be private to one or more users, or publicly available on the Web. When sharing a visualization as part of a Google application file, the entire file, and not just the visualization is shared to other users.

In any Google application that allows sharing, the **🔒 Share** button can be found in the upper right-hand corner of an open file or document. To share, click on this blue **Share** button in either a Spreadsheets or Fusion Tables file.

Private sharing

Sharing with Google applications can be public or private. This section details how to share a Spreadsheet or Fusion Table privately. In this scenario, to share privately means sharing to only a select group of individuals. Additionally, it is worth noting this information is universal across Google applications and thus can also be used to share files other than Spreadsheet or Fusion Tables documents.

Clicking on the blue **Share** button opens the **Share settings** window. The **Who has access** section indicates the overall privacy setting for the document as well as individual user access.

The global privacy setting has three options:

- Public on the Web
- Anyone with the link
- Private

To view or change the overall privacy setting, click on the **Change...** link. The **Sharing settings** window will appear. For allowing access to individuals, choose either the **Anyone with the link** or **Private** option to keep the file from being openly public on the Web. The **Anyone with the link** setting is technically publically accessible as there is no sign-in required. However the concept of "security through obscurity" is exercised here, as the link being shared will be somewhat random, not searchable, and assumedly not published on a separate publicly viewable website.

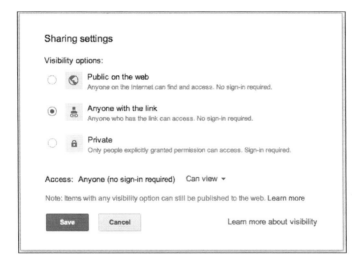

Google documents shared privately allow for individual user access control. From the **Sharing settings** window, enter the e-mail address(es) of the collaborator(s) in the **Add people** field.

Directly to the right of the **Add people** field, select the level of permissions the collaborator will have for the document from the drop-down menu.

Finally, decide if the newly added collaborator should be notified by e-mail of their new capabilities on the document. To notify the collaborator, select the **Notify people via email** checkbox. Add a personalized message to the notification e-mail if desired. Click on the **Share & save** button to save the newly configured share settings.

As a final configuration consideration, the collaborator's ability to freely add additional collaborators as well as change visibility options must be explored. On the main **Sharing settings** window, click on the **[Change]** link next to **Editors will be allowed to add people and change the permissions**.

In the **Sharing settings** window that appears, click on the desired permissions level for collaborators.

Sharing in Google documents is simple but not necessarily the best method of permanently publishing a visualization. This is particularly true when a standalone web page or web-embedded visualization is the goal. Google Docs does offer the option to open the document to all web users, but a specific drawback to sharing in this way is that the Google document itself is openly shared. Google Docs sharing is primarily a method of collaborative sharing to a small group, where as publishing a visualization as a web page is generally more desirable for wider audience viewing.

Public sharing

In general, Google documents can also be openly shared to everyone on the Web. A Google Doc shared to everyone results in anyone on the internet being able to view, comment on, or edit the file, depending on the permissions set. When a Google Doc is shared, anyone accessing the document is manipulating the actual Google file. This approach is useful for large collaborative document efforts, or when comments are desired in Google Doc format. It may, however, not be ideal for sharing to large audiences. Even though access can be limited to view only, an alternative method of sharing the Google Doc file itself is through publishing its content as a web page.

Publishing

Publishing a web version of a Visualization is distinctly different from sharing it via a Google Doc in that the web publication is standalone and is no longer a Google Doc file type. Therefore, efforts to secure the Visualization to a limited audience of viewers must be accomplished through the usual methods of security used on a standard website. However, manipulating the visualization on the published web page cannot modify the Google Doc, making it more appropriate for wider audience viewing. Web versions of a visualization can be created using Spreadsheets, Fusion Tables, or from scratch, and can be hosted by Google, or any web hosting service.

Spreadsheets

To publish a Google Spreadsheet and subsequent visualization to a web page, select from the menu, **File | Publish to the web...**.

From the **Publish to the web** window, if desired, configure the range of the Spreadsheet to be published. To create the live web version of the Spreadsheet, click on the [Start publishing] button. Once pressed, the website version of the Spreadsheet is available on the Web and can be reached by navigating a browser to the link given in the **Get a link to the published data** field. For a publication format other than a web page, click on the drop-down menu at the top of the **Get a link to the published data**. Alternative publication options available are as follows:

- Web page
- HTML to embed in a page
- CSV (comma-separated values)

- TXT (Plain Text)
- PDF (Adobe PDF)
- ATOM
- RSS

The following screenshot is of the web page version of the Spreadsheet for 2010 Chicago Census data. Note the similarity in appearance to the Spreadsheet file itself. However, the web version cannot be edited by site visitors and maintains a fairly static appearance in comparison to the Google Spreadsheets application.

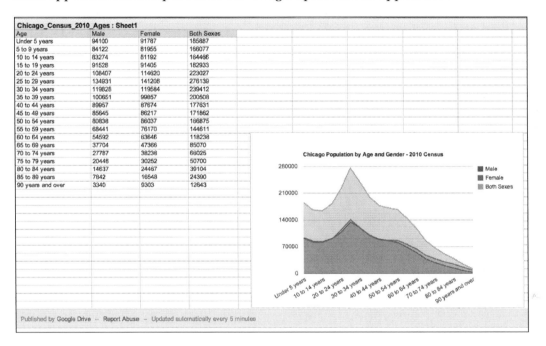

While data manipulation is not inherently available in the web version, limited mouse-over interactivity of the visualization is still available.

Fusion Tables

Publishing a web page from Fusion Tables is similar in process to publishing a web page from Spreadsheets. The primary difference is that each chart or component of the Fusion Table file is published individually. For example, a web page of table data is distinct from a chart web page, even when the two components are from the Fusion Tables document. To publish a component of a Fusion Table, select the component's tab and navigate to **Tools | Publish...** in the menu bar.

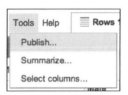

The **Publish** window will appear. Options for the method of publishing are displayed. The **Send a link in email or IM** produces a standalone, simple web page representation of the tab contents. Alternatively, the **Paste HTML to embed in a website** encapsulates the published component into an iFrame, allowing for easy addition as part of another page.

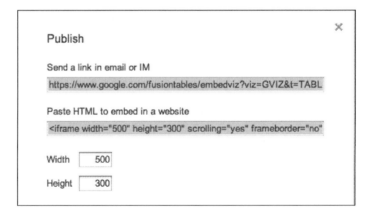

Web publication of a Google Doc is similar to sharing, but with distinct differences. Google provides additional information on the topic of sharing and web publishing for Google Docs in its support documentation.

 More information on Sharing versus Publish to Web Visibility is available at `https://support.google.com/drive/bin/answer.py?hl=en&answer=183965`.

Apps Script

Methods of standalone web publication for Apps Script files are also available. The publication process for both standalone and Spreadsheet-embedded App Scripts is mostly the same. The primary difference is that the Spreadsheet script may contain Spreadsheet-specific code, making it dependent on its respective Spreadsheet.

Publishing basics

The web publication of an Apps Script has two general steps. First, version management must be established before the Apps Script environment allows a script to be published. To initiate managed version control, click on **File | Manage Versions...** from the menu bar. In the **Manage Versions** window, enter a description of the version and click on **Save New Version**. The current script version will then be saved as a snapshot in time, and can be called on by other script projects. It can also be loaded as a particular instance of the published script.

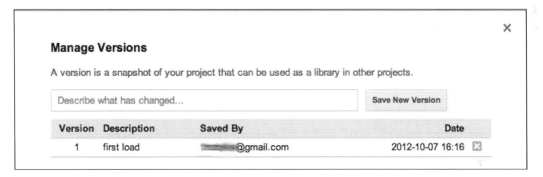

When at least one version is available, the Apps Script environment will allow a web instance to be published. From the menu bar, click on **Publish | Deploy as web app...** to deploy the script as a web page.

Alternatively, selecting the cloud arrow button from the menu bar also accesses the **Deploy as web app...** window.

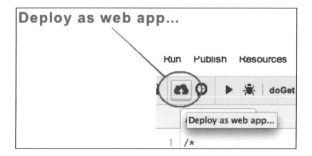

In the **Deploy as web app** window click on the script version that is to be deployed. The versions available are the same versions as saved in the **Manage Versions...** window. Next, select the level of access for the new web application. The **Execute this app as:** option tells the application under which user permissions to run the application. This setting is important because allowing a user to run as script developer allows the user to perform the same actions for which the developer has rights. However, certain normal actions in an application may require elevated permissions, thus potentially prohibiting the functionality of the script.

The **Who has access to the app:** setting is slightly more self-explanatory. This setting simply determines if web users can view the script application or if it is private to the developer.

 More information on Security and Google Apps Script is available at `https://developers.google.com/apps-script/scripts_google_accounts`.

Embedded in a Spreadsheet

Recall that designing an Apps Script that creates a visualization in a Spreadsheet requires programming specific to the Spreadsheet interface itself (see *Chapter 4, Basic Charts*). The result of this specification generally means an Apps Script attached to a Spreadsheet has a high chance of failing to translate into a standalone web page. Apps Scripts attached to a Spreadsheet are still fully functional and have the potential to stand alone as a web app, but any code referencing an interaction with the Spreadsheet must first be removed.

App Engine

There are various methods of launching applications on Google App Engine. Development of a visualization API application can be accomplished in just about any web development environment capable of handling HTML and JavaScript. The popular open source platform, Eclipse, can be used in its web development version with an added Google developer extension for seamless app deployment. Even simple text editors can be used to edit code when using the App Engine Launcher and Software Development Kit (SDK).

App Engine Launcher and SDK

The Google Development SDK provides the basic functionality needed to test and launch an application in App Engine. It is intended for use by developers fluent in Java, Python, or Google's own programming language, **Go**. A consequence of using the SDK method to publish API Visualizations is that there is some overhead programming required to create a Java, Python, or Go framework to serve HTTP pages. App Engine applications do however use the standard WAR structure for bundling web applications, making it possible to manually create an application folder structure.

In this method, testing and deploying the application is accomplished through the SDK command line or with the **GoogleAppEngineLauncher** tool.

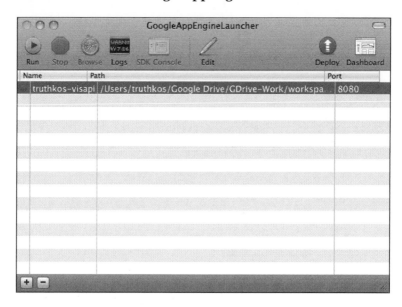

Eclipse plugin

If developing in an environment such as Eclipse, use the Google plugin for Eclipse. The plugin provides basic framework templates that are accessed as App Engine projects directly from Eclipse. Deployment of an App Engine application in Eclipse is as simple as with the Google plugin. After installing the plugin through the Eclipse add software method, create or deploy an App Engine application in Eclipse, and click on the 🔘 icon in the menu bar. From the drop-down menu, select the appropriate action desired.

For a new web project, the project initialization and configuration steps will look very similar to all other Eclipse project creation wizards.

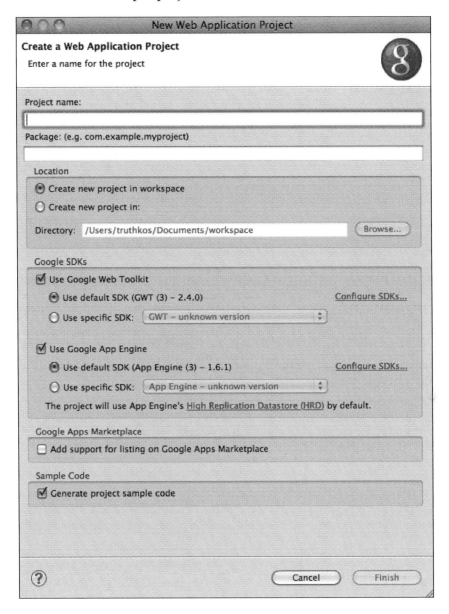

For more information on Eclipse, Google App Engine, and the Google Go programming language, visit the links listed here.

Eclipse development environment at `http://www.eclipse.org/`.

Google plugin for Eclipse at `https://developers.google.com/eclipse/`.

App Engine Developer downloads—SDK, Launcher, and Plugins at `https://developers.google.com/appengine/downloads`.

Google programming language: Go at `http://golang.org/`.

Integrated Development Environments in the Cloud (IDEs)

Possibly the most intuitive method of App Engine development is to use a cloud-based online development environment for which application deployment to App Engine is integrated. This approach allows for template-based deployment of App Engine apps as well as faster testing and update processes. Cloud 9 IDE (Integrated Development Environment) and Codenvy IDE are two popular cloud-hosted development environments available at the time of this book's publication. The Codenvy IDE is used in the following visualization API application example, with discussion of basic functionality as applied to launching visualization API applications in App Engine.

The Codenvy development application is fairly straightforward in organization. The menu bar is the primary access to environment functions. The folder structure of the application is on the left-hand side of the screen, with the selected file's contents displayed for editing on the right. The lower window and tabs display code previews and the output of environment operations, such as building and launching an application.

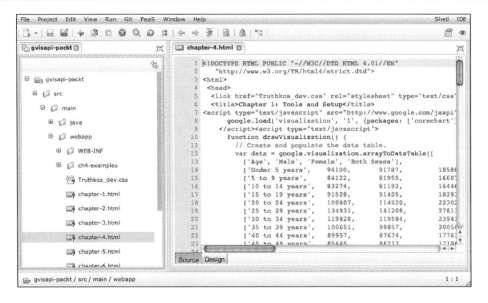

To create or update applications from the Codenvy IDE application, click on **PaaS | Google App Engine** from the menu bar. Choose either **Update Application** or **Create Application...** respectively.

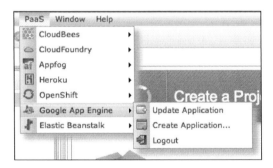

The Codenvy application will then guide the developer through the App Engine creating an application process or automatically updating an existing application on App Engine.

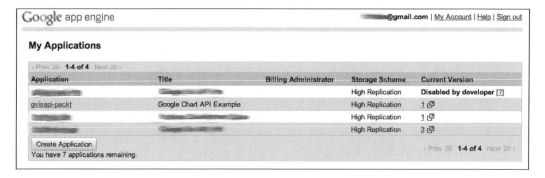

Much of the development and deployment process for App Engine is handled through the IDE. However, independent of the development environment, App Engine applications must be initially created in the App Engine console. As mentioned earlier, the creation of the Application ID is required when configuring an application to deploy from any of the deployment.

More APIs

In addition to the Visualization and Google Docs APIs, Google provides a selection of APIs for other Google services. While many of these APIs are available at no charge when consumed below a certain user threshold, heavier use requires a pay-for-what-you-use fee per API. To access additional APIs from Google, log in to the API Console. From the console, APIs can be turned on or off for a specific project.

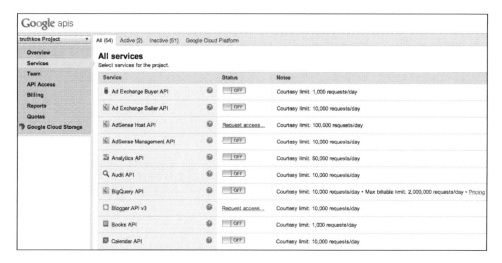

Publishing a Google Visualization as a web page allows for a variety of development and deployment options. These options are also diverse across developer experience levels and workflows, which makes visualizations easy to incorporate in existing websites or as standalone pages.

Information on Codenvy IDE is available at `https://codenvy.com/`.

Information on Cloud 9 IDE is available at `https://c9.io/`.

Information on API Console is available at `https://code.google.com/apis/console/`.

Project hosting on Google Code is available at `http://code.google.com/hosting/`.

A word on security

Ultimately the developer is responsible for maintaining a level of security assurance in visualized data. Google Visualizations, and any code that evokes the Google APIs for that matter, must be aware of the potential security risk that the use of an API on a data source creates. Google provides some guidance on this issue in their **Terms of Service** and **Program Policy**.

Security and data privacy with charts

Developers are responsible for abiding by the Google Terms of Service and Program Policy when publishing.

For more information please visit `https://google-developers.appspot.com/chart/interactive/docs/security_privacy`.

Summary

This chapter discussed the various methods of sharing and publishing a Google Visualization API application. Not only are the methods presented here applicable to Visualization API applications, but they can also be applied to other Google API-based applications. The Google Gadget publishing option was intentionally not covered in this chapter due to the uncertain future of the service. Additional information on Google Gadgets and the Gadgets API can be found at the following link:

Information on Gadgets API is available at
`https://developers.google.com/gadgets/`.

Overall, the Google Visualization API can be thought of as a "gateway" to learning all other Google APIs. It is simple enough for beginners, but can be used as part of more complex application design. The intention of this book has been to teach the breadth of possibilities of the Visualization API, while preparing the reader to engage more deeply with the Google development environment. As is true with all technology, particular details of visualization techniques may change. Yet, the methodology of learning how to interpret and apply the programmatic methods on which the Visualization API has been built is invaluable.

Index

Symbols

\<form\> tag 171

A

AllowHTML option 99
animated transitions 106
annotated timeline
  about 190
  charts 31
  coded version 192, 194
  event flags 191, 192
  spreadsheets 191
AnnotatedTimeLine 78
Anyone with the link setting 209
API 7
API Explorer 135
API framework
  about 143
  ChartWrapper 144
  ControlWrapper 144
API, static style option
  Cascading Style Sheets 95
  DataTable formatters 99, 100, 102
  formatters 93
  Inline 93
  views 96
App Engine
  about 217
  App Engine Launcher 217
  Eclipse plugin 218, 220
  IDEs in cloud 220-222
  more APIs 222, 223
  SDK 217

Application Programming Interface. *See* API
Apps Script
  about 215
  basics, publishing 215-217
  embedding, in Spreadsheet 217
  Framework 41, 42
  scripting console 42
  using 41
Apps Script Wrapper 80-82
AreaChart 75
array 68
array programming method 173
arrow formatter 100

B

BarChart 75
bar formatter 100, 102
bind function 160
Boolean 67
BubbleChart 75
Buckets tab 61

C

CandlestickChart 75
CategoryFilter control 159
cell formatting
  about 60
  info windows 62, 63
  lines 60
  markers 60
  polygon 60, 61
chart.draw() 26

Chart Editor
  about 38, 107, 176-178
  Chart styles 40
  Chart type function 38
  Chart types 39
  Configure data function 38
  reopening 40
  Style customization function 38
ChartEditor 79
chart formatting
  static style option 90
Charts
  data sources 126
Chart Tools Query Language 138
ChartWrapper
  about 26, 144
  data source 146
  draw 146, 147
  events 147
  load 145
  tasks 144
ChartWrapper class 177
ChartWrapper function 151
Chart Wrapper (wrapper.draw())
     method 107
classes 71
Clojure Language documentation 114
code conventions 73
Code Playground
  about 13, 14
  console 15, 16
  debugging tools 15
  Gadget Editor 16, 17
  links 15
color formatter 103
ColumnChart 75
ComboChart 76
conditional logic 70
constant variable 66
controls
  about 107, 150
  CategoryFilter 158-160
  ChartRangeFilter 160
  NumberRangeFilter 156, 157
  predictability 155, 156
  StringFilter 150-155
ControlWrapper method 150

D

dashboard
  about 107, 149, 150
  controls 150
  controls, with dependencies 161, 163
  filter by category 29
  Filter by chart range 28
  Filter by dependencies 29
  Filter by number range 28
  Filter by string 28
  programmatic control 163
  programmatic filtering 28
dashboardReady function 166, 168
data
  cleaning up 112, 113
  export options 114
  Facet 111
  importing 110
  preparing 110
data management
  about 48
  columns, modifying 49
  formula, adding 50
  rows, editing 48
  views 50, 51
  visualization, creating 52
data sources, for Charts
  building 139, 140
  Chart Tools Query Language 138
  spreadsheets 126
DataTable() class 117
DataTable formatters
  about 99
  arrow 100
  bar 100, 102
  color 103
  data 103
  number 104
  paging 105, 106
  pattern 104, 105
DataTable function 68, 118
date formatter 103
Document Object Model. *See* **DOM**
doGet function 81
DOM 203
DrawChart function 26, 73

draw function
setup process 147
drawVisualization function 84, 166

E

Eclipse 13
Edit button 112
Edit column option 113
equations
about 69
API call 69
attributes 69
conditional logic 70
loops 70
error event 147
events
about 29, 147
error 147
error handling 30
ready 147
ready for interaction 30
select 30, 148
sort 30
Event triggers 44
Execute this app as: option 216
experimental charts 54
Export button 114
export options 114

F

Facets 111, 112
feature mapping
about 55
cell formatting 60
geocoding 55
filterColumnLabel option 152
Firebug Lite Settings window 16
formatters 93
Freebase button 114
functions 70
Fusion Tables
about 11, 46
creating 11, 12
data, creating 46, 47
data, importing 46, 47

data management 48
facts 11
features, mapping 55
merging 52
new look 51
non-map visualizations 53
Fusion Tables API 126
Fusion Tables, Chart data sources
API Explorer 135, 136, 138
permission 133
preparation 132
query 133-135
URL path, obtaining 133
Fusion Tables, static style option
Chart Editor 92
Filters 92, 93

G

Gadget Editor
about 16, 17
facts 18
Gauge 79
geochart
about 79, 195, 197
code 199
ISO 3166 standard 197
marker option 197
setting requirements 197
spreadsheets 198, 199
geocoding
about 55
address method 57
data sources 56
errors, recognizing 58, 59
manual method 56, 57
third-party tools method 58
geomap
about 79, 195, 201
code 202, 203
marker option 196, 197
region option 196
Google App Engine 13
GoogleAppEngineLauncher tool 218
Google Drive Create tab 11
google.load command 142
Google Refine documentation 114

Google Spreadsheets
  about 124
  API 125
  forms 124, 125
Google Spreadsheets charts
  about 9
  creating 9, 10
  facts 9
Google Visualization Tools
  code playground 13
  Fusion Tables 11
  Google Spreadsheets charts 9
  interacting with 8
  knowledge, prerequisites 7
  scripting code 12
Google Web Tools plugin for Eclipse 13
Gradient tab 61
Graphic User Interface. *See* **GUI**
group 118
GUI 7, 35

H

handleQueryResponse function 130
HTML Framework 25

I

IDEs 220
ImageAreaChart 78
ImageBarChart 77
ImageCandlestickChart 77
ImageChart 77
ImageLineChart 78
ImagePieChart 78
ImageSparkLine 80
info window 62, 63
Integrated Development Environments. *See*
     IDEs
IntensityMap 79
interactive
  dashboard 27
  events 29
  time-based charts 31

J

join 120

joinMethod function 121
Jython Language documentation 114

K

key 119
Keyhole Markup Language. *See* **KML**
KML 55
knowledge, prerequisites
  about 7
  programming skills 8
  system requirements 8

L

libraries
  about 71
  commenting 72
  spacing/ format 73
LineChart 76
lines 60
Load API modules, chart types
  about 74
  AnnotatedTimeLine 78
  AreaChart 75
  BarChart 75
  BubbleChart 75
  CandlestickChart 75
  ChartEditor 79
  ColumnChart 75
  ComboChart 76
  Gauge 79
  GeoChart 79
  GeoMap 79
  ImageAreaChart 78
  ImageBarChart 77
  ImageCandlestickChart 77
  ImageChart 77
  ImageLineChart 78
  ImagePieChart 78
  ImageSparkLine 80
  IntensityMap 79
  LineChart 76
  MotionChart 79
  OrgChart 80
  PieChart 76
  ScatterChart 76
  SteppedAreaChart 77

Table 80
TreeMap 80
loops 70

M

major axis 98
Map API 203
maps
  about 195
  geochart 195
  geomap 195
Marathon route map 56
markers 60
medium format 103
minor axis 98
motion chart
  about 182-186
  code 188-190
  spreadsheets 186, 187
MotionChart 32, 79
multi-dimensional array 173

N

Navigation window 13
non-map visualizations
  about 53
  experimental charts 54
  simple line graph 53
null 68
number 67
number formatter 104

O

objects 71
Olympic Park map 56
onclick event 177
onclick() method 170
openEditor() function 177
OrgChart 80

P

PaaS | Google App Engine 221
packages 71
paging 105

pattern formatter 104
PieChart 76
polygon 60
programmatic control
  about 163-165
  global variables 165-169
programming concepts
  about 66
  classes 71
  functions 70
  libraries 71
  objects 71
  variables 66
publishing
  about 211
  App Engine 217
  Apps Script 215
  Fusion Tables 214
  options 212
  spreadsheet 212, 213
Publish window 214

R

ready event 147
responder function 148
run_on_event function 148

S

Scalable Vector Graphics. *See* SVG
ScatterChart 76
scripting code
  about 12
  facts 13
scripting code, Visualization API
  about 24
  chart.draw() 26
  ChartWrapper 26
  Draw.Chart() 26
  HTML Framework 25
  technique options 25
scripting console, Apps Script
  about 42
  App, publishing 44, 45
  event triggers 44
  function, testing 43

scripts, debugging 44
security
  charts, using 223
  more APIs 223
select event 148
Share settings window 208, 210
sharing
  about 207, 208
  private sharing 208-210
  public sharing 211
simple line graph 53
spreadsheets
  about 36
  Apps Script, using 41
  chart, creating 36, 37
  Chart Editor 38
spreadsheets, Chart data sources
  Apps Script method 132
  permissions 127
  preparation 126
  query 129-131
  URL path, obtaining 128, 129
static style option
  about 90
  API 93
  Fusion Tables 90, 91
  spreadsheets 90
SteppedAreaChart 77
string 67
SVG 195

T

Table chart 80
time-based charts
  about 31, 181
  annotated timeline 190
  annotated timeline charts 31
  motion chart 182-186
  motion charts 32
transition animation
  about 170, 171
  components 171
  programmatic switch 173
  User interface toggle 173
TreeMap 80

U

User interface toggle
  about 173
  Button behavior 174-176
  Create button 174

V

variables
  about 66
  array 68
  Boolean 67
  equations 69
  number 67
  String 67, 68
Vector Markup Language. *See* **VML**
Velodrome Information web page 56
views
  about 50, 96
  Axes options 97
  DataView, using 96
visualization
  Apps Script 86, 87
  creating 203, 204
  creating, steps 82
  Google Code Playground, using 83-86
Visualization API
  about 19
  Apps Script 21
  categories 26
  common structure 19, 20
  forms 21
  framework 22
  Fusion Tables 23
  scripting code 24
Visualization API, categories
  interactive 27
  static 27
Visualization API common Framework
  Apps Script Wrapper 80
  Load API modules 73, 74, 77-79
Visualization API data capabilities
  about 117
  group operation 118
  join 120-123

Visualization API-ready data sources 115
Visualization API Reference 65
visualization architecture
  API framework 143
  HTML framework 142
Visualize | Line 52
VML 195

W

Westminster Abbey web page 56
Who has access to the app
  setting 217

About Packt Publishing

Packt, pronounced 'packed', published its first book "*Mastering phpMyAdmin for Effective MySQL Management*" in April 2004 and subsequently continued to specialize in publishing highly focused books on specific technologies and solutions.

Our books and publications share the experiences of your fellow IT professionals in adapting and customizing today's systems, applications, and frameworks. Our solution based books give you the knowledge and power to customize the software and technologies you're using to get the job done. Packt books are more specific and less general than the IT books you have seen in the past. Our unique business model allows us to bring you more focused information, giving you more of what you need to know, and less of what you don't.

Packt is a modern, yet unique publishing company, which focuses on producing quality, cutting-edge books for communities of developers, administrators, and newbies alike. For more information, please visit our website: www.packtpub.com.

Writing for Packt

We welcome all inquiries from people who are interested in authoring. Book proposals should be sent to author@packtpub.com. If your book idea is still at an early stage and you would like to discuss it first before writing a formal book proposal, contact us; one of our commissioning editors will get in touch with you.

We're not just looking for published authors; if you have strong technical skills but no writing experience, our experienced editors can help you develop a writing career, or simply get some additional reward for your expertise.

NumPy Beginner's Guide
Second Edition

ISBN: 978-1-78216-608-5   Paperback: 284 pages

An action packed guide using real world examples of the easy to use, high performance, free open source NumPy mathematical library. Scientific computation with Python now made simpler.

1. Perform high performance calculations with clean and efficient NumPy code

2. Analyze large data sets with statistical functions

3. Execute complex linear algebra and mathematical computations

Matplotlib for Python Developers

ISBN: 978-1-84719-790-0   Paperback: 308 pages

Build remarkable publication quality plots the easy way

1. Create high quality 2D plots by using Matplotlib productively

2. Incremental introduction to Matplotlib, from the ground up to advanced levels

3. Embed Matplotlib in GTK+, Qt, and wxWidgets applications as well as web sites to utilize them in Python applications

4. Deploy Matplotlib in web applications and expose it on the Web using popular web frameworks such as Pylons and Django

Please check **www.PacktPub.com** for information on our titles

Sage Beginner's Guide

ISBN: 978-1-84951-446-0   Paperback: 364 pages

Unlock the full potential of Sage for simplifying and automating mathematical computing

1. The best way to learn Sage which is a open source alternative to Magma, Maple, Mathematica, and Matlab

2. Learn to use symbolic and numerical computation to simplify your work and produce publication-quality graphics

3. Numerically solve systems of equations, find roots, and analyze data from experiments or simulations

R Graphs Cookbook

ISBN: 978-1-84951-306-7   Paperback: 272 pages

Detailed hands-on recipes for creating the most useful types of graphs in R—starting from the simplest versions to more advanced applications

1. Learn to draw any type of graph or visual data representation in R

2. Filled with practical tips and techniques for creating any type of graph you need; not just theoretical explanations

3. All examples are accompanied with the corresponding graph images, so you know what the results look like

4. Each recipe is independent and contains the complete explanation and code to perform the task as efficiently as possible

Please check **www.PacktPub.com** for information on our titles

2311373R00150

Printed in Germany
by Amazon Distribution
GmbH, Leipzig